COBOL
FOR
DUMMIES®

Quick Reference

by John W. Fronckowiak

IDG
BOOKS
WORLDWIDE

IDG Books Worldwide, Inc.
An International Data Group Company

Foster City, CA ✦ Chicago, IL ✦ Indianapolis, IN ✦ Southlake, TX

COBOL For Dummies Quick Reference®

Published by
IDG Books Worldwide, Inc.
An International Data Group Company
919 E. Hillsdale Blvd.
Suite 400
Foster City, CA 94404
www.idgbooks.com (IDG Books Worldwide Web site)
www.dummies.com (Dummies Press Web site)

Library of Congress Catalog Card No.: 97-080870

ISBN: 0-7645-0247-6

Printed in the United States of America

10 9 8 7 6 5 4 3 2 1

1P/RV/RS/ZX/IN

Distributed in the United States by IDG Books Worldwide, Inc.

Distributed by Macmillan Canada for Canada; by Transworld Publishers Limited in the United Kingdom; by IDG Norge Books for Norway; by IDG Sweden Books for Sweden; by Woodslane Pty. Ltd. for Australia; by Woodslane Enterprises Ltd. for New Zealand; by Longman Singapore Publishers Ltd. for Singapore, Malaysia, Thailand, and Indonesia; by Simron Pty. Ltd. for South Africa; by Toppan Company Ltd. for Japan; by Distribuidora Cuspide for Argentina; by Livraria Cultura for Brazil; by Ediciencia S.A. for Ecuador; by Addison-Wesley Publishing Company for Korea; by Ediciones ZETA S.C.R. Ltda. for Peru; by WS Computer Publishing Corporation, Inc., for the Philippines; by Unalis Corporation for Taiwan; by Contemporanea de Ediciones for Venezuela; by Computer Book & Magazine Store for Puerto Rico; by Express Computer Distributors for the Caribbean and West Indies. Authorized Sales Agent: Anthony Rudkin Associates for the Middle East and North Africa.

For general information on IDG Books Worldwide's books in the U.S., please call our Consumer Customer Service department at 800-762-2974. For reseller information, including discounts and premium sales, please call our Reseller Customer Service department at 800-434-3422.

For information on where to purchase IDG Books Worldwide's books outside the U.S., please contact our International Sales department at 415-655-3200 or fax 415-655-3295.

For information on foreign language translations, please contact our Foreign & Subsidiary Rights department at 415-655-3021 or fax 415-655-3281.

For sales inquiries and special prices for bulk quantities, please contact our Sales department at 415-655-3200 or write to the address above.

For information on using IDG Books Worldwide's books in the classroom or for ordering examination copies, please contact our Educational Sales department at 800-434-2086 or fax 817-251-8174.

For press review copies, author interviews, or other publicity information, please contact our Public Relations department at 415-655-3000 or fax 415-655-3299.

For authorization to photocopy items for corporate, personal, or educational use, please contact Copyright Clearance Center, 222 Rosewood Drive, Danvers, MA 01923, or fax 508-750-4470.

About the Author

John W. Fronckowiak is president and founder of IDC Consulting, Inc., which specializes in Internet and intranet consulting, application development, and network consulting. He has extensive experience with database application development, client server networking, Internet and Intranet presence development, application development, and project management.

John currently holds degrees in Computer Science and Management Information Systems. He has performed a number of research projects using artificial intelligence and expert systems. He has also worked on projects involving creating large database data repositories and data mining of these repositories using neural networks.

John has been active on the Internet since the early '80s. He has helped a number of corporations get on the Web, including assisting businesses in developing their own intranets.

John lives in East Amherst, New York with his wife Diane and their cat Eiffel. John studies part time as a graduate student of Computer Science at the State University of New York at Buffalo. He is also a member of Mensa and is listed in *Who's Who In Media and Communications*.

John's previous writing experience includes *Building an Intranet For Dummies, Microsoft BackOffice 2 Unleashed, Microsoft BackOffice 2.5 Unleashed, Teach Yourself Database Programming With Visual J++ In 21 Days,* and *Teach Yourself OLE DB and ADO In 21 Days.* John also writes the Visual J++ Corner column for *Java Developers Journal.*

You can reach John on the Internet at john@buffnet.net.

ABOUT IDG BOOKS WORLDWIDE

Welcome to the world of IDG Books Worldwide.

IDG Books Worldwide, Inc., is a subsidiary of International Data Group, the world's largest publisher of computer-related information and the leading global provider of information services on information technology. IDG was founded more than 25 years ago and now employs more than 8,500 people worldwide. IDG publishes more than 275 computer publications in over 75 countries (see listing below). More than 60 million people read one or more IDG publications each month.

Launched in 1990, IDG Books Worldwide is today the #1 publisher of best-selling computer books in the United States. We are proud to have received eight awards from the Computer Press Association in recognition of editorial excellence and three from *Computer Currents'* First Annual Readers' Choice Awards. Our best-selling *...For Dummies®* series has more than 30 million copies in print with translations in 30 languages. IDG Books Worldwide, through a joint venture with IDG's Hi-Tech Beijing, became the first U.S. publisher to publish a computer book in the People's Republic of China. In record time, IDG Books Worldwide has become the first choice for millions of readers around the world who want to learn how to better manage their businesses.

Our mission is simple: Every one of our books is designed to bring extra value and skill-building instructions to the reader. Our books are written by experts who understand and care about our readers. The knowledge base of our editorial staff comes from years of experience in publishing, education, and journalism — experience we use to produce books for the '90s. In short, we care about books, so we attract the best people. We devote special attention to details such as audience, interior design, use of icons, and illustrations. And because we use an efficient process of authoring, editing, and desktop publishing our books electronically, we can spend more time ensuring superior content and spend less time on the technicalities of making books.

You can count on our commitment to deliver high-quality books at competitive prices on topics you want to read about. At IDG Books Worldwide, we continue in the IDG tradition of delivering quality for more than 25 years. You'll find no better book on a subject than one from IDG Books Worldwide.

John Kilcullen
CEO
IDG Books Worldwide, Inc.

Steven Berkowitz
President and Publisher
IDG Books Worldwide, Inc.

VIII
WINNER
Eighth Annual Computer Press Awards ≥1992

IX
WINNER
Ninth Annual Computer Press Awards ≥1993

WINNER

X
WINNER
Tenth Annual Computer Press Awards ≥1994

XI
WINNER
Eleventh Annual Computer Press Awards ≥1995

IDG Books Worldwide, Inc., is a subsidiary of International Data Group, the world's largest publisher of computer-related information and the leading global provider of information services on information technology. International Data Group publishes over 275 computer publications in over 75 countries. Sixty million people read one or more International Data Group publications each month. International Data Group's publications include: **ARGENTINA:** Buyer's Guide, Computerworld Argentina, PC World Argentina, **AUSTRALIA:** Australian Macworld, Australian PC World, Australian Reseller News, Computerworld, IT Casebook, Network World, Publish, Webmaster; **AUSTRIA:** Computerwelt Osterreich, Networks Austria, PC Tip Austria; **BANGLADESH:** PC World Bangladesh; **BELARUS:** PC World Belarus; **BELGIUM:** Data News; **BRAZIL:** Annuário de Informática, Computerworld, Connections, Macworld, PC Player, PC World, Publish, Reseller News, Supergamepower; **BULGARIA:** Computerworld Bulgaria, Network World Bulgaria, PC & MacWorld Bulgaria; **CANADA:** CIO Canada, Client/Server World, ComputerWorld Canada, InfoWorld Canada, NetworkWorld Canada, WebWorld; **CHILE:** Computerworld Chile, PC World Chile; **COLOMBIA:** Computerworld Colombia, PC World Colombia; **COSTA RICA:** PC World Centro America; **THE CZECH AND SLOVAK REPUBLICS:** Computerworld Czechoslovakia, Macworld Czech Republic, PC World Czechoslovakia; **DENMARK:** Communications World Danmark, Computerworld Danmark, Macworld Danmark, PC World Danmark, Techworld Denmark; **DOMINICAN REPUBLIC:** PC World Republica Dominicana; **ECUADOR:** PC World Ecuador; **EGYPT:** Computerworld Middle East, PC World Middle East; **EL SALVADOR:** PC World Centro America; **FINLAND:** MikroPC, Tietoverkko, Tietoviikko; **FRANCE:** Distributique, Hebdo, Info PC, Le Monde Informatique, Macworld, Reseaux & Telecoms, WebMaster France; **GERMANY:** Computer Partner, Computerwoche, Computerwoche Extra, Computerwoche FOCUS, Global Online, Macwelt, PC Welt; **GREECE:** Amiga Computing, GamePro Greece, Multimedia World; **GUATEMALA:** PC World Centro America; **HONDURAS:** PC World Centro America; **HONG KONG:** Computerworld Hong Kong, PC World Hong Kong, Publish in Asia; **HUNGARY:** ABCD CD-ROM, Computerworld Szamitastechnika, Internetto online Magazine, PC World Hungary, PC-X Magazin Hungary; **ICELAND:** Tolvuheimur PC World Island; **INDIA:** Information Communications World, Information Systems Computerworld, PC World India, Publish in Asia; **INDONESIA:** InfoKomputer PC World, Komputek Computerworld, Publish in Asia; **IRELAND:** ComputerScope, PC Live!; **ISRAEL:** Macworld Israel, People & Computers/Computerworld; **ITALY:** Computerworld Italia, Macworld Italia, Networking Italia, PC World Italia; **JAPAN:** DTP World, Macworld Japan, Nikkei Personal Computing, OS/2 World Japan, SunWorld Japan, Windows NT World, Windows World Japan; **KENYA:** PC World East African; **KOREA:** Hi-Tech Information, Macworld Korea, PC World Korea; **MACEDONIA:** PC World Macedonia; **MALAYSIA:** Computerworld Malaysia, PC World Malaysia, Publish in Asia; **MALTA:** PC World Malta; **MEXICO:** Computerworld Mexico, PC World Mexico; **MYANMAR:** PC World Myanmar; **NETHERLANDS:** Computer! Totaal, LAN Internetworking Magazine, LAN World Buyers Guide, Macworld Netherlands, Net, WebWereld; **NEW ZEALAND:** Absolute Beginners Guide and Plain & Simple Series, Computer Buyer, Computer Industry Directory, Computerworld New Zealand, MTB, Network World, PC World New Zealand; **NICARAGUA:** PC World Centro America; **NORWAY:** Computerworld Norge, CW Rapport, Datamagasinet, Financial Rapport, Kursguide Norge, Macworld Norge, Multimediaworld Norge, PC World Ekspress Norge, PC World Nettverk, PC World Norge, PC World ProduktGuide Norge; **PAKISTAN:** Computerworld Pakistan; **PANAMA:** PC World Panama; **PEOPLE'S REPUBLIC OF CHINA:** China Computer Users, China Computerworld, China InfoWorld, China Telecom World Weekly, Computer & Communication, Electronic Design China, Electronics Today, Electronics Weekly, Game Software, PC World China, Popular Computer Week, Software Weekly, Software World, Telecom World; **PERU:** Computerworld Peru, PC World Professional Peru, PC World SoHo Peru; **PHILIPPINES:** Click!, Computerworld Philippines, PC World Philippines, Publish in Asia; **POLAND:** Computerworld Poland, Computerworld Special Report Poland, Cyber, Macworld Poland, Networld Poland, PC World Komputer; **PORTUGAL:** Cerebro/PC World, Computerworld/Correio Informático, Dealer World Portugal, Mac*In*PC*In Portugal, Multimedia World; **PUERTO RICO:** PC World Puerto Rico; **ROMANIA:** Computerworld Romania, PC World Romania, Telecom Romania; **RUSSIA:** Computerworld Russia, Mir PK, Publish, Seti; **SINGAPORE:** Computerworld Singapore, PC World Singapore, Publish in Asia; **SLOVENIA:** Monitor; **SOUTH AFRICA:** Computing SA, Network World SA, Software World SA; **SPAIN:** Communicaciones World España, Computerworld España, Dealer World España, Macworld España, PC World España; **SRI LANKA:** Infolink PC World; **SWEDEN:** CAP&Design, Computer Sweden, Corporate Computing Sweden, Internetworld Sweden, it.branschen, Macworld Sweden, MaxiData Sweden, MikroDatorn, Nätverk & Kommunikation, PC World Sweden, PCAktiv, Windows World Sweden; **SWITZERLAND:** Computerworld Schweiz, Macworld Schweiz, PCtip; **TAIWAN:** Computerworld Taiwan, Macworld Taiwan, NEW ViSiON/Publish, PC World Taiwan, Windows World Taiwan; **THAILAND:** Publish in Asia, Thai Computerworld; **TURKEY:** Computerworld Turkiye, Macworld Turkiye, Network World Turkiye, PC World Turkiye; **UKRAINE:** Computerworld Kiev, Multimedia World Ukraine, PC World Ukraine; **UNITED KINGDOM:** Acorn User UK, Amiga Action UK, Amiga Computing UK, Apple Talk UK, Computing, Macworld, Parents and Computers UK, PC Advisor, PC Home, PSX Pro, The WEB; **UNITED STATES:** Cable in the Classroom, CIO Magazine, Computerworld, DOS World, Federal Computer Week, GamePro Magazine, InfoWorld, I-Way, Macworld, Network World, PC Games, PC World, Publish, Video Event, THE WEB Magazine, and WebMaster; online webzines: JavaWorld, NetscapeWorld, and SunWorld Online; **URUGUAY:** InfoWorld Uruguay; **VENEZUELA:** Computerworld Venezuela, PC World Venezuela; and **VIETNAM:** PC World Vietnam.   3/24/97

Dedication

For Sister Victoria Dickson, who believed in me at a very important time and also introduced me to the COBOL programming language.

Author's Acknowledgments

I would like to thank everyone who helped make this book possible.

To my wife Diane for putting up with me and helping me work through the day-to-day ups and downs while keeping me focused on my larger goals.

To the rest of my family — Mom, Dad, Kim, Mike, Marie, Mom S, Alicia, and Becky — for understanding and supporting my desire to write.

I'd also like to send special thanks to Studio B Productions, Inc., for presenting me with the opportunity to work on this project. To David Rogelberg, who believed in me and my abilities and thought I would be a good fit for this project. And especially to Brian Gill who provided an immeasurable amount of assistance in working through the many details of this project — I could never handle them on my own.

Thanks also goes to Ellen Camm for giving me the opportunity to write this book, and to Mary Goodwin, my Project Editor. In addition, thanks go to all the unseen individuals who helped turn this book into reality.

Finally, thanks to my cat Eiffel and my Quaker parrot Elmo for providing companionship (and loud meows and squawks) while I wrote this book.

Publisher's Acknowledgments

We're proud of this book; please register your comments through our IDG Books Worldwide Online Registration Form located at: http://my2cents.dummies.com.

Some of the people who helped bring this book to market include the following:

Acquisitions, Development, and Editorial

Project Editor: Mary Goodwin

Acquisitions Editor: Ellen Camm

Copy Editor: John C. Edwards

Technical Editor: Jeff Lagasse

Editorial Managers: Mary C. Corder and Elaine Brush

Editorial Assistant: Paul Kuzmic

Production

Project Coordinator: Sherry Gomoll

Layout and Graphics: Maridee V. Ennis, Brent Savage, M. Anne Sipahimalani, Kate Snell

Proofreaders: Chris H. Collins, Michelle Croninger, Rachel Garvey, Nancy Price, Janet M. Withers

Indexer: Sherry Massey

General and Administrative

IDG Books Worldwide, Inc.: John Kilcullen, CEO; Steven Berkowitz, President and Publisher

IDG Books Technology Publishing: Brenda McLaughlin, Senior Vice President and Group Publisher

Dummies Technology Press and Dummies Editorial: Diane Graves Steele, Vice President and Associate Publisher; Mary Bednarek, Acquisitions and Product Development Director; Kristin A. Cocks, Editorial Director

Dummies Trade Press: Kathleen A. Welton, Vice President and Publisher; Kevin Thornton, Acquisitions Manager; Maureen F. Kelly, Editorial Coordinator

IDG Books Production for Dummies Press: Beth Jenkins, Production Director; Cindy L. Phipps, Manager of Project Coordination, Production Proofreading, and Indexing; Kathie S. Schutte, Supervisor of Page Layout; Shelley Lea, Supervisor of Graphics and Design; Debbie J. Gates, Production Systems Specialist; Robert Springer, Supervisor of Proofreading; Debbie Stailey, Special Projects Coordinator; Tony Augsburger, Supervisor of Reprints and Bluelines; Leslie Popplewell, Media Archive Coordinator

Dummies Packaging and Book Design: Patti Crane, Packaging Specialist; Lance Kayser, Packaging Assistant; Kavish + Kavish, Cover Design

◆

The publisher would like to give special thanks to Patrick J. McGovern, without whom this book would not have been possible.

◆

Contents at a Glance

Table of Contents

How to Use This Book

Welcome to *COBOL For Dummies Quick Reference*, the only quick reference you need when it comes to working with COBOL.

You've found exactly the right book if you want a quick and handy way to look up the answers to those COBOL questions that wake you up in the middle of the night.

About This Book

COBOL For Dummies Quick Reference is a fast and easy guide to the 85 COBOL (ANSI Standard X.3.23-1985) programming language. The book includes an overview of COBOL, a review of file types, a flow chart reference, a guide to planning for and solving the year-2000 problem in legacy applications, and a guide to forming syntactically-correct COBOL statements.

In *COBOL For Dummies Quick Reference,* I tell you everything you need to know about each COBOL division — the IDENTIFICATION DIVISION, ENVIRONMENT DIVISION, DATA DIVISION, and PROCEDURE DIVISION. I spell out each division's keywords and commands in alphabetical order, and I provide examples when I think they may help you see things more clearly.

COBOL For Dummies Quick Reference provides COBOL programming advice in a format where you can find just what you need to know — quickly and efficiently, without rummaging through unnecessary information.

Who Are You?

The first thing you need to know about this book is that it doesn't show you COBOL programming from the ground up — if you're a COBOL beginner, and you need a slow walk through the programming language, you should turn to *COBOL For Dummies,* published by IDG Books Worldwide, Inc., by Arthur Griffith, for more basic information.

This book offers an excellent refresher for programmers who have previously used COBOL. This book also serves as an excellent reference for COBOL programmers who are in the middle of developing an application and can't quite remember the specific syntax, command, or structure they should use.

How to Use This Book

COBOL For Dummies Quick Reference fits nicely between your computer and your coffee cup, making it easy to keep the book within arm's reach when you need an answer to a COBOL question.

To find out what you need to know, you should probably start with the index. The Table of Contents also can help you find topics in the book — a quick scan shows that I organize topics alphabetically within the parts, making it even easier for you to find the information you need.

What Are All These Parts?

COBOL For Dummies Quick Reference is divided into the following 12 parts:

Part I: Getting to Know COBOL. This part provides an introduction to the COBOL programming language, including a review of basic concepts, an overview of the ANSI standard COBOL revisions, and a guide to Internet sites with COBOL-related information.

Part II: The IDENTIFICATION DIVISION. Turn to Part II to get quick and easy answers about the IDENTIFICATION DIVISION, which is the part of a COBOL program that allows you to tell the user something about your program.

Part III: The ENVIRONMENT DIVISION. In this part, I show you both sections — the CONFIGURATION and INPUT-OUTPUT SECTIONS — of the ENVIRONMENT DIVISION in detail.

Part IV: The DATA DIVISION. You can find all the answers to your questions about the DATA DIVISION in this part, which covers the FILE, WORKING STORAGE, LINKAGE, COMMUNICATION, and REPORT SECTIONS of the division.

Part V: The PROCEDURE DIVISION. You may find yourself consulting this part frequently to remember the different parts of the PROCEDURE DIVISION, because this is where most of the work in your COBOL programs gets done.

Part VI: COBOL Verbs. Just like the verbs in a sentence, COBOL verbs make things happen in your programs. Turn to this part for a quick review of the standard COBOL verbs.

Part VII: Working with Files. This part provides a review of the different types of files provided by COBOL, including Sequential, Relative, Indexed, Sort-Merge, and Report files. I also give you an overview of platform-specific file details.

Part VIII: The Flowchart Reference. Many legacy applications use flowcharts. In this part I provide a quick review and reference to understanding these flowcharts, including a complete list of the most common symbols used in the charts.

Part IX: Debugging Your Application. When you need help remembering the concepts and keywords necessary in the debugging of your COBOL applications, consult this part.

Part X: Compiler Considerations and CICS. This part lets you in on the special considerations and concepts related to creating COBOL applications on different computing architectures.

Part XI: Solving The Year 2000 Problem. The time is upon you — you need to start updating your legacy programs for the year 2000. Visit this part for some hints about how to get started.

Part XII: COBOL Formats. Part XII gives you an overview of the syntax and structure of the COBOL programming language.

A Field Guide to the Funny Icons

Indicates an important fact or procedure you need to keep in mind.

Points out a nifty time saver or shortcut.

Oooops! You want to watch out for these. These icons indicate potential pitfalls and how to steer clear of them.

When I think an example can help me get my point across, I provide one for you, and I stick one of these icons next to it so that you can find the examples quickly.

When you see this icon, a feature specific to ANSI-85 COBOL is explained.

Other Stuff You Should Know

I use the following conventions throughout the code in this book:

✦ Reserved words are always capitalized.

✦ Required keywords are all capitalized and **bold**.

✦ If a keyword is not in bold, it is optional.

✦ When there is a choice of a series of phrases, they are surrounded by curly braces, {}, and phrases are separated by *or*.

✦ When items are enclosed in braces, one of the enclosed items must be used.

✦ An ellipsis (…) indicates that further information may be included, usually by repeating the preceding element any number of times.

Please note that the italicized *or* is not part of the COBOL programming language but is simply used to separate choices.

✦ Optional phrases are enclosed in brackets, [].

Keep In Touch

I love to hear from readers. Please let me know what you liked in this book, disliked, or would like to see more of. You can contact me through e-mail at john@buffnet.net.

Part I

Getting to Know COBOL

If you're already familiar with the COBOL programming language, you may want to skip this part. But wait! In addition to showing you the nuts and bolts of COBOL, this part also details the differences between the last two major COBOL standards (ANSI-74 COBOL and ANSI-85 COBOL). I also give you a quick review of the features to look forward to in ANSI-97 COBOL.

In this part . . .

- ✔ Getting to know the differences between ANSI-74 COBOL and ANSI-85 COBOL

- ✔ Looking towards the future of COBOL with ANSI-97 features

- ✔ Surfing the Internet for cool COBOL Web sites

- ✔ Using the different areas of the COBOL source code line

- ✔ Putting your COBOL programs in the correct order

ANSI Standards

ANSI (the American National Standards Institute) helps engineering societies and a number of government agencies develop voluntary consensus standards. ANSI also helps promote and assess compliance to those standards.

COBOL adheres to the ANSI standardization process, and a number of ANSI-standard versions of COBOL have popped up over the years. Today, programmers recognize two major ANSI revisions:

+ **The ANSI-74 standard:** Also known as COBOL 74

+ **The ANSI-85 standard:** Also known as COBOL 85

Almost all COBOL compilers currently conform to the ANSI-85 COBOL standard.

You should write applications which conform to ANSI-85 standards as much as possible to provide the best chance for cross-platform compatibility. You may find it hard to always conform to ANSI-85 standards, due to compiler restrictions or application requirements. When you break away from the ANSI-85 standards, you should clearly document these areas of your application.

COBOL Versions

Many versions of COBOL are still in use, and a new version is already in the works. A knowledge of the differences between some of these versions may help you update your applications — and help you know what to expect in the future for COBOL programming.

Comparing COBOL 74 and 85

If you're not dealing with the conversion of older ANSI-74 COBOL programs to ANSI-85 COBOL, then you can skip this section.

The following list details the substantive changes in ANSI-85 COBOL:

+ The ENVIRONMENT DIVISION is optional.

+ The CONFIGURATION SECTION is optional.

+ The SOURCE-COMPUTER paragraph is optional.

+ The OBJECT-COMPUTER paragraph is optional.

♦ The SPECIAL-NAMES paragraph has undergone many changes:

- If an implementor-name is a switch, a condition name is not required.

- The IS phrase is optional.

- STANDARD-2 is a new entry.

- The CURRENCY SIGN literal must be non-numeric and one character long.

- The sorting sequence of an indexed file is the same as the native character set in use when the file was created.

- ALPHABET is required in the alphabet-name clause.

♦ The FILE-CONTROL paragraph has changed quite a bit:

- The ASSIGN clause can now use a non-numeric literal.

- OPTIONAL can now be used with relative and indexed files when they are opened in Input, I-O, or extended mode.

- The ORGANIZATION IS phrase is optional.

- CODE-SET can now be specified for sequential files.

- The RECORD DELIMITER and PADDING clauses have been added.

♦ The order of clauses in the I-O CONTROL paragraph is no longer important.

♦ The DATA DIVISION is optional.

The following features in the file and data description section are new to ANSI-85 COBOL:

♦ You can omit the BLOCK CONTAINS clause without specifying a physical record size.

♦ The LABEL RECORD clause is optional; STANDARD is now the default.

♦ Data names in the LINAGE clause can be qualified; files with the LINAGE clause can't be opened with the EXTEND mode.

♦ The EXTERNAL and GLOBAL clauses are new to the file and data description sections.

♦ The FILLER clause is optional.

♦ When using the OCCURS clause, the data item in the DEPEND-ING ON phrase can be zero.

- ✦ A PICTURE string can be continued on another line; a period or comma can now be the last character in a PICTURE string if it is followed by a separator.

- ✦ Field positions designated by a P contain zeroes when a MOVE is executed and the source is numeric and contains a P. When a MOVE is executed and the source is numeric (or numeric edited) and contains a P and the destination is numeric (or numeric edited), both operands of a comparison are numeric.

- ✦ The VARYING phrase has been added to the RECORD clause.

- ✦ If a FOOTING is not specified in the LINAGE clause, no end-of-page condition exists.

- ✦ A zero can be specified as the relative line number in the PLUS phrase of the LINE-NUMBER clause.

- ✦ The word following a level indicator, level number 01, or level number 77 can begin in Area A.

- ✦ When using the REDEFINES clause, the size of an item can be less than or equal to the size of the item being redefined.

- ✦ A RELATIVE KEY clause data item can't have a P in its PICTURE statement.

- ✦ Multiple SIGN clauses can appear in an entry; the SIGN clause can appear in a report group description entry.

- ✦ The SIGN IS SEPARATE clause must be used for signed numeric data items when the file description or file control entry contains the CODE SET clause.

- ✦ If the SIGN clause is specified in a report group description, it must be with the SEPARATE CHARACTER phrase.

- ✦ SYNCHRONIZED can be used with INDEX data items.

- ✦ The USAGE clause now has BINARY and PACKED-DECIMAL options.

- ✦ The VALUE clause can be specified for an item with an OCCURS clause.

Other differences in ANSI-85 COBOL include the following features:

- ✦ The PROCEDURE DIVISION is optional.

- ✦ Non-numeric literals can now be up to 160 characters long.

- ✦ Up to 50 levels of qualification are provided.

+ Tables can have up to seven dimensions. Tables can also have relative subscripting. (Subscripts and indices can be mixed.)

+ User-defined words can be the same as system names; a user-defined word must only be unique if it is referenced in the program.

+ Sequence numbers can contain any character.

+ When a comma or semicolon is followed by a space, you can simply replace the comma or semicolon with a space.

+ The I-O status item has new values.

+ The communication status key has new values, and the communication error key has been added.

+ In the communication description entry, the order of statements is no longer important, and the I-O phrase has been added.

+ The DEBUG-ITEM description has changed.

+ When using the class condition, the ALPHABETIC test is for both upper and lowercase letters and space.

+ Conditional statements are evaluated from left to right. As soon as the logical value is determined, the evaluation stops.

+ A data item in the USING phrase of a PROCEDURE DIVISION header can't have a REDEFINES clause in its description.

+ The PROGRAM-ID paragraph can now use the COMMON and INITIAL phrases.

+ ZERO can now be used in arithmetic expressions.

+ The relationship operators IS GREATER THAN OR EQUAL TO and IS LESS THAN OR EQUAL TO have been added.

The following important changes have been made to COBOL verbs:

+ CANCEL closes all open files.

+ When using the CLOSE command, the NO REWIND phrase can't be used if the REEL/UNIT phrase is specified.

+ When using the DIVIDE command, any subscripting for the REMAINDER identifier is evaluated after the result has been stored in the GIVING identifier.

+ When the EXIT PROGRAM command is called, all PERFORMS are terminated.

✦ When the MERGE command is called, the two files can't be in a SAME AREA or SAME SORT-MERGE AREA clause.

✦ Using the OPEN command with the I-O or extend mode causes a file to be created if it doesn't already exist.

✦ When using the READ command, there are limits on the INTO phrase.

✦ There are new restrictions on the INTO phrase of the RETURN command.

✦ The GIVING phrase of the SORT command can have multiple files.

✦ The STOP RUN command closes all open files.

✦ When using the WRITE command, ADVANCING PAGE and END-OF-PAGE can't be used simultaneously.

COBOL 97

ANSI-85 COBOL is by no means the final version of the programming language; a proposal for an ANSI-97 COBOL standard is in the works and should become accepted and implemented just after the turn of the century.

Some of the anticipated changes in ANSI-97 COBOL include:

✦ Continued development and standardization of objects, inheritance, and methods (Many COBOL compilers already support varying levels of object orientation.)

✦ More intrinsic functions

✦ Features to increase the internationalization of the language

✦ Extensions to the CALL and EXIT statements

✦ Bit, Boolean, and floating point data types

COBOL Information on the Internet

Even though COBOL is a language born out of the hippie '60s generation, and this is the '90s — the dawn of the new millennium — you can still find tons of information about this dinosaur language on the Internet, including the following Web sites:

✦ **COBOL Center:** www.infogoal.com/cbd/cbdhome.htm

✦ **COBOL Foundation:** www.cobol.org/

- **COBOL Gold Mine:** www.ils-international.com/ilsintl/welcome.htm

- **COBOL Homepage:** www.yi.com/home/HegartyJohn/cobol/index.html

- **COBOL Programming and Information:** home1.gte.net/stinnett/

- **MVSHelp.COM:** www.mvshelp.com

- **National Committee for Information Technology Standards:** www.x3.org/

- **PC Webopaedia:** www.sandybay.com/pc-web/COBOL.htm

You can also visit the COBOL newsgroup at comp.lang.cobol for a discussion of the COBOL programming language and software.

A number of major companies produce ANSI-85 standard COBOL compilers for a variety of computer platforms. These companies include the following:

- **Acucobol, Inc.:** www.acucobol.com/

- **Amdahl:** orpheus.amdahl.com/doc/products/oes/cb.uts/cobolftr.html

- **Computer Associates:** www.cai.com/products/addbm/cobol.htm

- **Digital Equipment Corporation:** ww1.systems.digital.com/

- **Fujitsu:** www.adtools.com

- **IBM COBOL:** www.software.ibm.com/ad/cobol/cobol.htm

- **MicroFocus, Inc.:** www.microfocus.com/

- **NiGSuN International:** www.nigsun.es

- **Ryan McFarland - Liant:** www.liant.com

Column Areas

If you're working through old legacy applications, you may encounter a pile of coding forms, which look like the following figure:

COBOL Coding Form

SYSTEM			PUNCHING INSTRUCTIONS				PAGE 1 OF 3
PROGRAM LABELS			GRAPHIC			CARD	IDENTIFICATION
PROGRAMMER		DATE FEB '81	PUNCH			FORM #	73 80

```
010010 IDENTIFICATION DIVISION.
010020 PROGRAM-ID. LABELS.
010030 ENVIRONMENT DIVISION.
010050
010060 CONFIGURATION SECTION.
010070 SOURCE-COMPUTER. ABC 480.
010080 OBJECT-COMPUTER. ABC 480.
010090
010100 INPUT-OUTPUT SECTION.
010110 FILE-CONTROL.
010120     SELECT ADDRESS-FILE ASSIGN TO CARD-READER.
010130     SELECT PRINT-FILE   ASSIGN TO PRINTER.
010140
010150 DATA DIVISION.
010160
010170 FILE SECTION.
010180
010190 FD ADDRESS-FILE
010200    LABEL RECORDS ARE OMITTED
010210    DATA RECORD IS ADDRESS-RECORD.
010220 01 ADDRESS-RECORD.
010230    02 NAME              PIC X(25).
010240    02 STREET            PIC X(25).
```

Some COBOL implementations still use the standard 80-column format of the original punch cards; refer to your specific compiler to determine any line-length restrictions.

Coding forms helped a programmer ensure that information was placed in the appropriate column. While programmers no longer use punch cards, most COBOL application editors still identify the column areas.

Every COBOL program includes four important areas. Because no one ever thought of more interesting names, programmers call these areas

  ✦ **Sequence area**

  ✦ **Indicator area**

  ✦ **Area A**

  ✦ **Area B**

Sequence area

The first six characters, columns 1 through 6, of every line are used for an optional sequence number. A sequence number labels a source program line.

Sequence numbers don't need to be unique, and they also don't need to be in any particular order. Sequence numbers simply identify individual lines in an application by the compiler.

Indicator area

Column 7, called the *indicator area*, controls continuation. If a source code line can't fit on a single line, you can continue the source code line by placing a hyphen (-) in the indicator area.

Column 7 also indicates that a line contains a comment entry (*see also* Part V for more information on comments). If you place an asterisk (*) in the indicator area, the compiler ignores any text you enter on that line. You can also place a forward slash (/) in column 7 to indicate that a comment follows, but when the source program goes to the printer, a new page command is sent after the comment is printed.

Finally, column 7 can also contain a debug directive (if the directive contains a D). Debugging lines must be syntactically and logically correct, or the compiler can't compile your application.

You can continue debugging lines by placing another D in column 7 of the next line. (*See also* Part IX for more information on debugging.)

Area A

Area A occupies character positions 8, 9, 10, and 11. All new paragraphs and section names must begin in Area A.

Area B

Area B begins at column 12 and stretches to the end of the line (the total number of characters allowed per line depends on your COBOL compiler). Basically, the bulk of your source code begins in Area B; everything except for paragraph and section names begins in this area.

Formatting and Rules

COBOL is a long winded and highly structured programming language. Like every programming language, you need to understand a certain set of rules to program in COBOL.

Separators

A *separator* is a character delimiting a character string. Use any of the following characters as a separator:

✦ A sequence of one or more spaces (called a *separator space*)

✦ A sequence of one comma followed by one or more spaces

✦ A sequence of one semicolon followed by one or more spaces

✦ A sequence of one period followed by one or more spaces

✦ A left parenthesis

✦ A right parenthesis

✦ A quotation mark indicating the start of a literal value

✦ A quotation mark indicating the end of a literal value

✦ A colon

✦ The pointer qualification symbol (->)

✦ The concatenation operator (&)

Words

A COBOL *word* is a single character string consisting of COBOL character-set characters. COBOL offers the following types of words:

✦ **User-defined words:** The names of all user-defined words except level-numbers must be unique.

✦ **System-name:** A system-name links the program with the operating system. A system-name can be either a user-specified word or a specific word.

✦ **Reserved:** A reserved word is a specific word for process writing in a program.

✦ **Function-name:** A function-name is a word indicating the name of a function.

COBOL words have the following general restrictions:

✦ A COBOL word must not exceed 30 characters in length.

✦ A COBOL word must be made up of alphabetic characters (A to Z and a to z), numeric characters (0 to 9), or hyphens (-). Lowercase letters are regarded as being equivalent to their corresponding uppercase letters. A word can't contain any spaces. A user-defined word may consist of national characters.

✦ You can't use a hyphen as the first or last character of a COBOL word.

Literals

A *literal* is a value that is directly written into a program. COBOL offers two primary types of literals:

✦ **Numeric literals:** A numeric literal contains 1 to 18 numeric characters. It can include a decimal point and an algebraic sign. If a sign is present, it must be the leftmost character. If a sign is not present, the value is positive. The decimal point can't be the last character.

✦ **Non-numeric literals:** A non-numeric literal is a character string delimited by quotation marks (""). It can be up to 160 characters long. (Previously the length limit of non-numeric literals was 120 characters.) A non-numeric literal can contain any character in the systems character set.

To embed a quote in a non-numeric literal, use two consecutive quotation marks. For example, the literal — I said, "Do you like green eggs and ham?" — would be written like this: ""I said, "Do you like green eggs and ham?"""

Nesting Programs

ANSI-85 COBOL allows you to nest programs within other COBOL programs. (Nested programs can reference some of the resources of the programs where they are contained.)

Division headers

In a nested program, you indicate the beginning of a division by the division header. You indicate the end of a division with another division header or an end-program header. You can use any of the following recognized division headers:

```
IDENTIFICATION DIVISION.
ENVIRONMENT DIVISION.
DATA DIVISION.
PROCEDURE DIVISION [USING {data-name-1}. . .].
```

The framework of a nested program

The following example illustrates the framework of nested programs:

```
IDENTIFICATION DIVISION.
PROGRAM-ID. PROGRAM-A.

    IDENTIFICATION DIVISION.
    PROGRAM-ID. PROGRAM-B.
    END PROGRAM PROGRAM-B.
```

```
IDENTIFICATION DIVISION.
PROGRAM-ID. PROGRAM-C.

   IDENTIFICATION DIVISION.
   PROGRAM-ID. PROGRAM-D.
   END PROGRAM PROGRAM-D.

END PROGRAM PROGRAM-C.

END PROGRAM PROGRAM-A.
```

In this example, PROGRAM-B, PROGRAM-C, and PROGRAM-D are all nested in PROGRAM-A. PROGRAM-B and PROGRAM-C are directly contained in PROGRAM-A. PROGRAM-D is indirectly contained in PROGRAM-A, because it is first contained within PROGRAM-C.

Names

While the difference between a directly and indirectly nested program may seem nit-picky, you need to make the distinction when determining the scope of names defined by a program. Programmers usually call PROGRAM-A the *common program,* because it's the main controlling program where all other programs are nested.

The *scope* of a name is the area within a program where it's valid to use that name. Programs which are nested in another program can use identical user-defined words to specify items, no matter how the program it's nested in already uses that word.

You can't use certain names outside of the program where they are declared. These include communication description names, paragraph names, and section names. Any program can use library and text names.

A program name, such as PROGRAM-B, can only be referenced by the CALL or CANCEL statements (***see also*** PART VI for a complete reference of the CALL and CANCEL statements). When a program is nested within another program, it can only be referenced by the program it's contained in, or any other programs that are directly contained within the common program.

When referencing data items, unless the data items are declared as global, they can only be used in the program where they are defined. If a data item is referenced, and it's not declared in the program where it is being referenced, the compiler searches the nesting program for the reference next. This search continues until the common program is reached.

Ordering Your Program

COBOL is a highly structured and ordered programming language. Beyond the specific formatting and rules of the COBOL programming language, you need to also understand and follow a higher order of program structure.

COBOL programs break up into four major divisions: the IDENTI- FICATION, ENVIRONMENT, DATA, and PROCEDURE DIVISIONS.

In versions of the COBOL programming language prior to the ANSI-85 standard, each of these divisions was required in all programs. In the ANSI-85 COBOL standard, the ENVIRONMENT, DATA and PROCEDURE DIVISIONS are now optional, which means that a valid COBOL program can just consist of the IDENTIFICATION DIVISION.

In most cases, a program that consists only of the IDENTIFICA- TION DIVISION wouldn't help you very much. However, such a program can help you when you're developing nested programs. You can identify the nested programs with just the IDENTIFICA- TION DIVISION during the early compilation testing/debugging development phase, and then fill in the rest of the program body as your programming proceeds.

IDENTIFICATION DIVISION

The IDENTIFICATION DIVISION is the first mandatory division of all COBOL programs. The IDENTIFICATION DIVISION provides the name of the source program. You can also include other optional documentary information, such as the program author, where the program is installed, when it was written, when it was compiled, and any applicable security restrictions.

See also Part II for more information on the IDENTIFICATION DIVISION.

ENVIRONMENT DIVISION

The ENVIRONMENT DIVISION specifies the aspects of a particular program that depend on specific hardware. The ENVIRONMENT DIVISION defines the following items:

+ The character set used by your program

+ The collating sequence used by your program

+ Associate function and mnemonic names

✦ Symbolic-constants, symbolic-characters, and alphabet-names

✦ Associate files with platform-specific devices and actual file names

See also Part III for more information on the ENVIRONMENT DIVISION.

DATA DIVISION

The DATA DIVISION defines the data used by the program, the hierarchical relationships of the data, and condition names.

The DATA DIVISION contains two sections: the FILE and WORK-ING-STORAGE sections:

✦ **The FILE section:** Defines the name of the file, the name of each record, the hierarchical structure of the data elements in the file, and the size and type of each data element. (*See also* Part VII for more information on COBOL files and file types.)

✦ **The WORKING-STORAGE section:** Defines non-file related data elements used by your programs, such as counters and temporary storage areas.

See also Part IV for more information on the DATA DIVISION.

PROCEDURE DIVISION

The heart of a COBOL program lies in the PROCEDURE DIVISION, where all the actual work gets done and procedures are defined.

Procedures are a sequence of instructions or commands that are executed in order. These commands or instructions are called *verbs* in the COBOL programming language. Typically these verbs perform a set of actions using the files and variables defined by the program.

See also Part V for more information on the PROCEDURE DIVISION and Part VI for more information on COBOL verbs.

Part II

The IDENTIFICATION DIVISION

The IDENTIFICATION DIVISION provides the name of the source program and any other optional documentary information, such as the program author, where the program is installed, when it was written, when it was compiled, and any applicable security restrictions.

Documentation is an essential aspect of any well written program. The IDENTIFICATION DIVISION provides a means for COBOL programmers to provide basic, standardized documentation for all their programs.

You can also use comments to specify most of the information in the IDENTIFICATION DIVISION. In the early days of COBOL, the IDENTIFICATION DIVISION included some mandatory documentation for applications. Everything in the IDENTIFICATION DIVISION except for the program name is now optional.

This part describes the syntax and function of all the paragraphs provided in the IDENTIFICATION DIVISION.

In this part . . .

✔ **Understanding the division's format**

✔ **Naming your COBOL program**

✔ **Providing standard documentation in your COBOL programs**

Acquainting Yourself with the Division's Format

The words IDENTIFICATION DIVISION must begin in Area A and be followed by a period.

The general format of the IDENTIFICATION DIVISION is:

```
IDENTIFICATION DIVISION.
    PROGRAM ID program-name-1
        [IS {COMMON | INITIAL} PROGRAM].
    [AUTHOR. [comment-1] ...]
    [INSTALLATION. [comment-2] ...]
    [DATE-WRITTEN. [comment-3] ...]
    [DATE-COMPILED. [comment-4] ...]
    [SECURITY. [comment-5] ...]
```

In the ANSI-85 COBOL standard, only the PROGRAM ID paragraph is required; all other paragraphs will be obsolete in the ANSI-97 COBOL standard.

AUTHOR

The AUTHOR paragraph is an optional paragraph which tells who wrote the program. You only include it for documentation purposes, and the AUTHOR paragraph does not affect how the program executes. (ANSI-97 COBOL won't offer the AUTHOR paragraph at all.)

Check out the following star-studded example of the AUTHOR paragraph:

```
AUTHOR. John Fronckowiak.
```

Unless your name is John-Jacob-Jingle-Heimmer-Schmidt, you probably don't have to worry about your name continuing over more that one line. If the author's name does need to run over more than one line, feel free to continue the name on multiple lines and just wrap things up with a period once you're done.

DATE-COMPILED

The DATE-COMPILED paragraph is an optional paragraph which identifies when the program was compiled. You only include this paragraph for documentation purposes, and it does not affect how the program executes. (ANSI-97 COBOL won't offer the DATE-COMPILED paragraph at all.)

The date a program was compiled can be useful when you're trying to keep track of multiple versions of the same program.

Take a look at an example of a DATE-COMPILED paragraph in action:

```
DATE-COMPILED. August 21, 1979.
```

You can continue the DATE-COMPILED paragraph on more than one line; however, you can't continue it with a hyphen. To continue the DATE-COMPILED paragraph on multiple lines, just make the paragraph as long as you want, and then end it with a period.

DATE-WRITTEN

The DATE-WRITTEN paragraph is an optional paragraph which identifies when the program was written. You include it only for documentation purposes, and it does not affect how the program executes. (ANSI-97 COBOL won't offer the DATE-WRITTEN paragraph at all.)

The date a program was written can be useful when you're trying to keep track of multiple versions of the same program.

The following code shows you a prime example of a DATE-WRITTEN paragraph:

```
DATE-WRITTEN. August 15, 1979.
```

The DATE-WRITTEN paragraph can continue on more than one line; however it can't be continued with a hyphen. To continue the DATE-WRITTEN paragraph on multiple lines, just type the paragraph and end it with a period.

INSTALLATION

The INSTALLATION paragraph is an optional paragraph which identifies the location where the program has been installed (or the location of the computer, company, or whatever else your heart desires because it doesn't effect how your program runs). You included it only for documentation purposes, and it does not affect how the program executes. (ANSI-97 COBOL won't offer the INSTALLATION paragraph at all.)

Ready to see an example of the INSTALLATION paragraph? Behold:

```
INSTALLATION. IDC Consulting Inc.
```

The INSTALLATION paragraph can continue on more than one line; however, you can't continue it with a hyphen. To continue the INSTALLATION paragraph on multiple lines, just type the paragraph and end it with a period.

PROGRAM ID

The PROGRAM ID paragraph names the program source, object, and any other associated files. The PROGRAM ID paragraph is the only mandatory section of the IDENTIFICATION DIVISION.

The format of the PROGRAM ID paragraph is:

```
PROGRAM ID program-name [IS {COMMON | INITIAL} PROGRAM].
```

The *program-name* must conform to user-defined word specification (*see also* Part I for additional information about identifiers).

If the program is contained within another program (*see also* Part I for additional information on nesting programs), each program name must be unique.

The COMMON and INITIAL parameters are new features in ANSI-85 COBOL. Only one of these parameters can be specified for each program. The COMMON parameter can be specified only if the program is contained within another program.

Common programs can only be called from other nested programs. Common programs can't call themselves.

If the INITIAL parameter is specified, each time the program is called, it, and any nested programs it contains, are set to their initial state. Any data items which are contained in this program or any other nested programs are set to their initial state as specified by the VALUE IS clause.

The following code shows a typical PROGRAM ID paragraph:

```
PROGRAM ID. ACCOUNTING-PROG-1.
```

For your viewing pleasure, the following code shows you a PROGRAM ID paragraph which utilizes the INITIAL option:

```
PROGRAM ID. ACCOUNT-PROG-1 IS INITIAL PROGRAM.
```

SECURITY

The SECURITY paragraph is an optional paragraph which identifies any applicable program security restrictions. You include it only for documentation purposes, and it does not affect how the program executes. (ANSI-97 COBOL won't offer the SECURITY paragraph at all.)

You can use the SECURITY paragraph to identify which users should be allowed access to the program.

The following example shows you what a SECURITY paragraph looks like:

```
SECURITY. This program is restricted to A Level
          personnel.
```

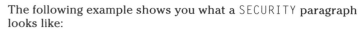

The SECURITY paragraph can continue on more than one line, however, you can't continue it with a hyphen. To continue the SECURITY paragraph on multiple lines, just type the paragraph and end it with a period.

Part III

The ENVIRONMENT DIVISION

The ENVIRONMENT DIVISION breaks down into two sections, the CONFIGURATION SECTION and the INPUT-OUTPUT SECTION. This part describes the syntax and function of all the paragraphs provided in the ENVIRONMENT DIVISION.

In this part . . .

✔ Defining alphabets, special characters, class-names, and implementor names using the CONFIGURATION SECTION

✔ Using the INPUT-OUTPUT SECTION to access files

✔ Controlling how you access files and devices

Acquainting Yourself with the Division's Format

The ENVIRONMENT DIVISION is the second division of all COBOL programs. The ENVIRONMENT DIVISION specifies the aspects of a particular program that depend on certain hardware. Specifically, the ENVIRONMENT DIVISION defines:

+ The character set used by your program

+ The collating sequence used by your program

+ Associate function and mnemonic names

+ Symbolic-constants, symbolic-characters, and alphabet-names

+ Associate files with platform specific devices and actual file names

In versions prior to ANSI-85 COBOL, the ENVIRONMENT DIVISION was a mandatory division, but in ANSI-85 COBOL, it is optional.

CONFIGURATION SECTION

The CONFIGURATION SECTION has five purposes:

+ It describes the *source computer* (the computer that will compile the program) and the *object computer* (the computer that will run the program).

+ It defines the currency sign, decimal point, and other symbol characters used by the program.

+ It defines *class-names,* which describe a set of characters.

+ It defines a relationship between implementor names and mnemonic names.

+ It defines alphabet names which relate to character sets or sorting orders.

To begin the CONFIGURATION SECTION, the words CONFIGURATION SECTION must be typed in Area A and followed by a period.

The CONFIGURATION SECTION has the following format:

```
[CONFIGURATION SECTION.

[SOURCE-COMPUTER. [computer-name-1
        [WITH DEBUGGING MODE].]]
```

```
[OBJECT-COMPUTER. [computer-name-2
[MEMORY SIZE integer-1 {WORDS or CHARACTERS or MODULES}]
[PROGRAM COLLATING SEQUENCE IS alphabet-name-1]
[SEGMENT-LIMIT IS segment-number].]]

[SPECIAL-NAMES. [[implementor-name-1
 {IS mnemonic-name-1
   [ON STATUS IS condition-name-1
[OFF STATUS IS condition-name-2]] or
IS mnemonic-name-2
[OFF STATUS IS condition-name-2
[ON STATUS IS condition-name-1]] or
ON STATUS IS condition-name-1
[OFF STATUS IS condition-name-2] or
OFF STATUS IS condition-name-2
[ON STATUS IS condition-name-1]}]]...
  [ALPHABET alphabet-name-1 IS
    {STANDARD-1 or
     STANDARD-2 or
     NATIVE or
     implementor-name-2 or
     {literal-1
       [{THROUGH or THRU} literal-2 or
       {ALSO literal-3}...]}...]}...
  [SYMBOLIC CHARACTERS {symbolic-character-1}...
    {IS or ARE} {integer-1}...}...
    [IN alphabet-name-2]]...
  [CLASS class-name-1 IS {literal-4
    [{THROUGH or THRU} literal-5]}...]...
[CURRENCY SIGN IS literal-6]
[DECIMAL POINT IS COMMA].]]]
```

When programs are nested (***see also*** Part I for more information
about program nesting), they can't have a CONFIGURATION
SECTION. The entries in the CONFIGURATION SECTION of the
main program are shared with all other nested programs.

OBJECT-COMPUTER

In ANSI-85 COBOL the OBJECT-COMPUTER section is now optional.
(In previous ANSI COBOL versions, the OBJECT-COMPUTER
section was required.)

The OBJECT-COMPUTER section describes the hardware where the
program is run. The name of the object computer is not required
to be the same as the source computer name.

You need to review your COBOL compiler and system-specific
documentation for the list of computer names valid for your
system.

The OBJECT-COMPUTER section has the following format:

```
[OBJECT-COMPUTER. [computer-name-1
[MEMORY SIZE integer-1 {WORDS or CHARACTERS or MODULES}]
[PROGRAM COLLATING SEQUENCE IS alphabet-name-1]
[SEGMENT-LIMIT IS segment-number].]]
```

The MEMORY SIZE clause defines the amount of memory needed for the program to run. If you don't have enough memory to run your application, each system responds differently.

While MEMORY SIZE is still part of the ANSI-85 COBOL standard, it is scheduled to be removed from future versions. It's a holdover from the days of extremely limited system memory — today, most desktop computers have more system memory than the common mainframe of 10 to 15 years ago.

The PROGRAM COLLATING SEQUENCE clause defines the default alphabet used when sorting character-related information. This alphabet is used by default with the SORT and MERGE commands unless another alphabet is explicitly specified.

If the PROGRAM COLLATING SEQUENCE is not specified, the system default collating sequence is used. Consult your compiler and system-specific documentation for more information on alphabets you can use.

The SEGMENT-LIMIT clause is an obsolete clause. While it is still included in the ANSI-85 COBOL standard, it is scheduled to be removed from future versions. The segment number specified must have a value of 01 to 49; these segments (or areas of memory) are considered permanent while your application runs.

SOURCE-COMPUTER

In ANSI-85 COBOL, the SOURCE-COMPUTER section is now optional. (In previous ANSI COBOL versions the SOURCE-COMPUTER section was required.)

The SOURCE-COMPUTER section defines the system where the program is compiled. (The source computer and object computer can be different. The source computer is where your program is compiled, and the object computer is where your program will execute.)

The SOURCE-COMPUTER section has the following format:

```
[SOURCE-COMPUTER. [computer-name
     [WITH DEBUGGING MODE].]]
```

If you include the WITH DEBUGGING phrases, all debugging sections and lines are compiled. (*See also* Part IX for more information on debugging your COBOL programs.)

If the WITH DEBUGGING clause is not included, all debugging lines and sections are treated just like comments — like they aren't there.

SPECIAL-NAMES

All the action in the CONFIGURATION SECTION occurs in the SPECIAL-NAMES section. The SPECIAL-NAMES section associates implementor names with mnemonic names and conditions, defines alphabets, defines symbolic characters, creates class conditions, and specifies the default decimal point and currency symbols.

To begin the SPECIAL-NAMES section, type the words SPECIAL NAMES and then a period in Area A.

When using the SPECIAL-NAMES section to associate an implementor name with a mnemonic name, use the following format:

```
[[implementor-name-1
 {IS mnemonic-name-1
   [ON STATUS IS condition-name-1
   [OFF STATUS IS condition-name-2]]}]...
```

An *implementor name* is a system name associated with a device. The device can control a switch, or be an input or output device like a card reader or printer. The device can be used with the ACCEPT, DISPLAY, SEND, and WRITE commands, but it can't have any condition names associated with it (***see also*** Part V for more information about conditions and condition names).

The ON and OFF status clauses associate a condition name with the current device status. You need to refer to your COBOL compiler and system-specific documentation for a list of system-supported devices.

The following code provides an example of an implementor name definition:

```
ENVIRONMENT DIVISION.
  SPECIAL-NAMES.
* Associate MY-PRINTER with the system device
* SYS-PRINTER.
    MY-PRINTER IS SYS-PRINTER.
```

ALPHABET

The ALPHABET clause defines the standard character sorting sequence used by your program, which is the character sorting sequence that's used by default with the SORT and MERGE commands, unless another sorting sequence is specified.

The ALPHABET clause has the following format:

```
[ALPHABET alphabet-name-1 IS
    {STANDARD-1 or
    STANDARD-2 or
    NATIVE or
    implementor-name-2 or
    {literal-1
        [{THROUGH or THRU} literal-2 or
        {ALSO literal-3}...]}...}]...
```

You can define more than one alphabet name using the ALPHABET clause. You can associate an alphabet name with any one of the following four types of standard alphabets :

♦ When the STANDARD-1 alphabet is specified, the standard ANSI ASCII character set is used. (The STANDARD-1 alphabet clause is new to ANSI-85 COBOL.)

♦ When the STANDARD-2 alphabet is specified, the International Standards Organization character set is used. (The STANDARD-2 alphabet clause is new to ANSI-85 COBOL.)

♦ When the NATIVE clause is specified, the default system character set is used.

♦ When the implementor-named character set is used, a character set defined by the system is used. You need to consult with your COBOL compiler and system-specific documentation to determine if your system supports system-defined character sets.

The THROUGH, THRU, or ALSO clauses are used for user-defined character sets. The THROUGH or THRU clause defines a contiguous range of character from the native system character set. The ALSO clause adds additional characters to the range.

The following example demonstrates how to define an alphabet name:

```
ENVIRONMENT DIVISION.
* Define MY-ALPHA-1 as the standard alphabet, and
* MY-ALPHA-2 as just capital letters.
SPECIAL-NAMES.
    ALPHABET MY-ALPHA-1 IS STANDARD-1
    ALPHABET MY-ALPHA-2 IS "A" THRU "Z".
```

SYMBOLIC CHARACTERS

The SYMBOLIC CHARACTERS clause associates a name with a character position in a character set. (The SYMBOLIC CHARACTERS clause is new to the ANSI-85 COBOL standard.)

The SYMBOLIC CHARACTERS clause has the following format:

```
[SYMBOLIC CHARACTERS {symbolic-character-1}...
    {IS or ARE} {integer-1}...}...
    [IN alphabet-name-2]]...
```

The following example demonstrates how to use the SYMBOLIC CHARACTERS clause:

```
ENVIRONMENT DIVISION.
* Associate the name AMPERSAND with the 38th character
* in the standard character set.
    SPECIAL-NAMES.
            SYMBOLIC CHARACTERS
                AMPERSAND IS 38
                IN STANDARD-1.
```

If you want to associate the name AMPERSAND with the & character in the STANDARD-1 character, first determine the position of the & character in the ASCII character set. To save you the effort of figuring that out, I'll tell you that it's the 38th character.

CLASS

When defining a CLASS condition, the condition is considered to be true if the data item being tested contains only the characters defined by the class name. A class name is defined in the SPECIAL NAMES section of the ENVIRONMENT DIVISION (*see also* "SPECIAL NAMES" in this part for more information on class names).

The CLASS entry has the following format:

```
[CLASS class-name-1 IS {literal-4
    [{THROUGH or THRU} literal-5]}...]...
```

The following example code demonstrates how to define a class name condition:

```
ENVIRONMENT DIVISION.
* Define the class name binary, for data items that
* only contain ones and zeros.
    SPECIAL-NAMES.
            CLASS BINARY IS 0 THROUGH 1.
```

The default currency sign

You can use the SPECIAL NAMES section to define the symbol used as the default currency symbol and to make the default decimal point a comma instead of a period. These sections have the following format:

```
[CURRENCY SIGN IS literal-6]
[DECIMAL-POINT IS COMMA]
```

The literal value used to specify the currency symbol must be only one character long. It can't be any of the following letters: a through z, 0 through 9, A, B, C, D, P, R, S, V, X, Z, *, +, (, -,), /, =, comma, period, semicolon, quotation character, or space.

In the ANSI-85 COBOL standard, the currency symbol can now be an L, which was not allowed in previous versions.

If the CURRENCY and DECIMAL-POINT clauses are not included, the default currency symbol becomes the dollar sign ($), and a period decimal point is used.

The following code demonstrates how to change the currency symbol to an L, and how to use the comma as a decimal point:

```
ENVIRONMENT DIVISION.
* Make L the default currency symbol, and comma the
* default decimal point.
   SPECIAL-NAMES.
      DECIMAL-POINT IS COMMA
         CURRENCY SIGN IS "L".
```

INPUT-OUTPUT SECTION

The INPUT-OUTPUT SECTION associates system file names and devices with program file names, defines the physical location of files, and defines characteristics of the devices where the files are stored.

The INPUT-OUTPUT SECTION is comprised of two parts:

+ **File Control section:** Associates system filenames and devices with program filenames, including the format and structure of the file.

+ **I-O Control section:** Defines the location of files and attributes of the storage devices associate with the files used.

To begin the INPUT-OUTPUT SECTION, type the words INPUT-OUTPUT SECTION followed by a period in Area A.

The INPUT-OUTPUT SECTION has the following format:

```
[INPUT-OUTPUT SECTION.
FILE-CONTROL.
{file-control-entry}...

[I-O-CONTROL.
  [[RERUN [ON {file-name-1 or
              implementor-name-1}]EVERY}
     {{END OF {REEL or UNIT} or
     integer-1 RECORDS} OF file-name-2 or
     integer-2 CLOCK-UNITS or
     condition-name-1}]...
```

```
[SAME
  [RECORD or
   SORT or
   SORT-MERGE] AREA FOR file-name-3
                          {file-name-4}...]...
  [MULTIPLE FILE TAPE CONTAINS
   {file-name-5 [POSITION integer-3]}...]....]]]]
```

FILE-CONTROL

The FILE-CONTROL SECTION associates a program name with
an external file. A file control entry or SELECT statement defines
and describes each file; file control entry or SELECT statement
appears for each file used by the program.

The format of the FILE-CONTROL entry depends on the type of file
accessed. A file control entry can describe any of the five following
file types:

- ✦ **Sequential file:** In a sequential file, the records are written in
  serial order and are read in the same order as written.

- ✦ **Relative file:** A relative file is one in which records are
  accessed by reference to their relative position in the file.

- ✦ **Indexed file:** An indexed file is something of a balance
  between sequential file organization and relative file organization. It allows sequential storage but also allows the same
  random accessing or processing of relative files.

- ✦ **Sort-merge file:** A sort-merge file contains a collection of
  records to be sorted or merged. A sort-merge file is created
  when, not surprisingly, you call the SORT or MERGE commands. The sort-merge file acts as a temporary storage area; it
  can't be accessed outside of the SORT or MERGE commands.

- ✦ **Report file:** A report file is a sequential output file defined by
  the REPORT clause. A report file consists of records that are
  written by the Report Writer Control System.

Each file type has a different file control entry format:

```
SEQUENTIAL FILE:

SELECT [OPTIONAL] file-name-1
    ASSIGN TO {implementor-name-1 or literal-1}...
    [RESERVE integer-1 [AREA or AREAS]]
    [[ORGANIZATION IS] SEQUENTIAL]
    [PADDING CHARACTER IS {data-name-1 or literal-2}]
        [RECORD DELIMITER IS
         {STANDARD-1 or implementor-name-2}]
    [ACCESS MODE IS SEQUENTIAL]
    [FILE STATUS IS data-name-2].
```

```
RELATIVE FILE:

SELECT [OPTIONAL] file-name-1
    ASSIGN TO{implentor-name-1 or literal-1}...
    [RESERVE integer-1 [AREA or AREAS]]
    [[ORGANIZATION IS] [RELATIVE]
        [ACCESS MODE IS
            {SEQUENTIAL [RELATIVE KEY IS data-name-1] or
            {RANDOM or
             DYNAMIC}
             RELATIVE KEY IS data-name-1}]
    [FILE STATUS IS data-name-2].

INDEXED FILE:

SELECT [OPTIONAL] file-name-1
    ASSIGN TO{implentor-name-1 or literal-1}...
    [RESERVE integer-1 [AREA or AREAS]]
    [[ORGANIZATION IS] INDEXED
    [ACCESS MODE IS
        {SEQUENTIAL or RANDOM or DYNAMIC}]
        RECORD KEY IS data-name-1
        [ALTERNATE RECORD KEY IS data-name-2
        [WITH DUPLICATES]]...
    [FILE STATUS IS data-name-3].

SORT OR MERGE FILE:

  SELECT file-name-1 ASSIGN TO
{implentor-name-1 or literal-1}....

REPORT FILE:

SELECT [OPTIONAL] file-name-1
    ASSIGN TO{implentor-name-1 or literal-1}...
    [RESERVE integer-1 [AREA or AREAS]]
    [[ORGANIZATION IS] SEQUENTIAL]
    [PADDING CHARACTER IS {data-name-1 or literal-2}]
        [RECORD DELIMITER IS
            {STANDARD-1 or implementor-name-2}]
    [ACCESS MODE IS SEQUENTIAL]
    [FILE STATUS IS data-name-2].
```

The following code shows you an example of the most basic file control entry:

```
FILE-CONTROL.
* Assign MY-FILE to the file MY-FILE.DAT
    SELECT MY-FILE ASSIGN TO "MY-FILE.DAT".
```

The ASSIGN phrase is the only required phrase of the SELECT statement. The name following the ASSIGN phrase is the name of the file or device associated with the filename identifier.

The other clauses of the SELECT statement are optional; they define the structure and organization of the file:

✦ The OPTIONAL phrase can only be used with input, input-output, and extended type files.

In versions before the ANSI-85 COBOL standard, the OPTIONAL phrase could only be used with sequential input files. If the OPTIONAL phrase is included, the actual file described does not need to be present when the application begins.

An example of a file control entry which uses the OPTIONAL phrase follows:

```
FILE-CONTROL.
* Assign MY-FILE to the file MY-FILE.DAT, make sure
* MY-FILE is optional.
  SELECT OPTIONAL MY-FILE
      ASSIGN TO "MY-FILE.DAT".
```

✦ The RESERVE phrase determines the number of areas allocated to a file. Each area is a file buffer. The RESERVE phrase is followed by an integer, which determines the number of buffers allocated at run time for the file.

If the RESERVE phrase is not included, the system you use dictates the number of areas reserved.

An example of a file control entry which uses the RESERVE phrase follows:

```
FILE-CONTROL.
* Assign MY-FILE to the file MY-FILE.DAT, reserving
* 10 areas
  SELECT MY-FILE
      ASSIGN TO "MY-FILE.DAT"
      RESERVE 10 AREAS.
```

✦ The ORGANIZATION phrase specifies the file organization used by the file. The ORGANIZATION phrase can be followed by either the SEQUENTIAL, RELATIVE, or INDEXED identifiers.

If the ORGANIZATION phrase is not included, a sequential file type is assumed.

An example of a file control entry which uses the ORGANIZATION phrase follows:

```
FILE-CONTROL.
  * Assign MY-FILE to the Relative file MY-FILE.DAT
  SELECT MY-FILE
  ASSIGN TO "MY-FILE.DAT"
  ORGANIZATION IS RELATIVE.
```

+ The PADDING phrase specifies the character used when filling unused character positions between records in a sequential file. (The PADDING phrase is new to the ANSI-85 COBOL standard.) The literal or contents of the data name used must be one character long.

An example of a file control entry which uses the PADDING phrase follows:

```
FILE-CONTROL.
* Assign MY-FILE to the file MY-FILE.DAT, using *
* as the record padding character
    SELECT MY-FILE
        ASSIGN TO "MY-FILE.DAT"
        PADDING IS "*".
```

+ The RECORD DELIMITER phrase determines the length of a variable sized record. The RECORD DELIMITER phrase can be followed by STANDARD-1 or an implementor name.

The STANDARD-1 phrase can only be used if the file is stored on a tape device. You should refer to your COBOL compiler and system-specific documentation for implementor names supported by your system.

+ The ACCESS MODE phrase determines the way files are accessed from the file. This is not the way the file is physically organized; it's the order which records are read from the file. The ACCESS MODE phrase can be followed by either the SEQUENTIAL, RANDOM, or DYNAMIC identifier.

If SEQUENTIAL mode is specified, then the records are read in the order they were written if the file is organized as sequential, or in sorted key order if the file organization is relative or indexed.

If RANDOM mode is specified, records can be accessed in any order. The RANDOM access mode can only be used with relative and indexed type files.

If DYNAMIC mode is specified, the file can be accessed either sequentially or randomly. The DYNAMIC access mode can only be used with relative and indexed type files.

If the RELATIVE KEY phrase is also included in the access mode, the data name that follows identifies the relative key data item used to access records in files with relative organization. The RELATIVE KEY phrase can only be used with relative type files.

The following example shows a file control entry which uses the ACCESS MODE phrase:

```
FILE-CONTROL.
* Assign MY-FILE to the indexed file MY-FILE.DAT, using
* KEY-1 as the primary key for random access
    SELECT MY-FILE
        ASSIGN TO "MY-FILE.DAT"
            ACCESS MODE IS RANDOM
        ORGANIZATION IS INDEXED
        RECORD KEY IS KEY-1.
```

✦ The RECORD KEY phrase identifies the primary key data item for indexed type files; it is mandatory when describing indexed files. The key identifies a data element which is unique for each record — for example, a customer number or order number.

The following example shows you a file control entry which uses the RECORD KEY phrase:

```
FILE-CONTROL.
* Assign MY-FILE to the indexed file MY-FILE.DAT, using
* KEY-1 as the primary key
    SELECT MY-FILE
        ASSIGN TO "MY-FILE.DAT"
        ORGANIZATION IS INDEXED
        RECORD KEY IS KEY-1.
```

✦ The ALTERNATE RECORD KEY phrase specifies an alternate key which can be used to access records in indexed type files. If the DUPLICATE phrase follows, the alternate key does not need to be unique.

The ALTERNATE RECORD KEY phrase can be used to access files with multiple keys. An alternate key must be an alphanumeric data item described in the record entry description of the file — it can't be a group item. If the file contains variable length records, the alternate key must be contained within the fixed area of the record. If a file was created using multiple alternate keys, they all must be used every time the file is referenced.

An alternate key can't be contained within a primary key data item.

✦ The STATUS phrase associates a data item with the I-O status of a file. (*See also* Part IV for more information on I-O status values.)

I-O-CONTROL

The I-O-CONTROL section specifies how files are stored on a device. Some of the storage attributes in this section are specifically designed for files stored on tape devices.

The I-O-CONTROL section has the following format:

```
[I-O-CONTROL.
 [[RERUN [ON {file-name-1 or
              implementor-name-1}] EVERY}
  {{END OF {REEL or UNIT} or
  integer-1 RECORDS} OF file-name-2 or
  integer-2 CLOCK-UNITS or
  condition-name-1}]...
 [SAME
   [RECORD or
    SORT or
    SORT-MERGE] AREA FOR file-name-3
                        {file-name-4}...]...
 [MULTIPLE FILE TAPE CONTAINS
   {file-name-5 [POSITION integer-3]}...]....]]]]
```

While the MULTIPLE FILE and RERUN phrases are supported in ANSI-85 COBOL, they are scheduled to be removed from future versions. In the ANSI-85 COBOL standard, these phrases can appear in any order.

The RERUN phrase specifies where the program stores rerun information. You can use the RERUN phrase in seven different ways:

+ **RERUN EVERY END OF REEL *or* UNIT OF *file-name*:** Causes rerun information to be stored on the filename specified, which must be a sequential file opened for output.

+ **RERUN ON *file-name-1* EVERY END OF REEL *or* UNIT OF *file-name-2*:** Causes rerun information to be written on filename-1, which must be open as an output file. *File-name-2* must be a sequential file opened for output.

+ **RERUN ON *implementor-name* EVERY END OF REEL *or* UNIT OF *file-name*:** Causes rerun information to be stored on the device defined by implementor name. *File-name* must be a sequential file opened for output.

+ **RERUN ON *implementor-name* EVERY *integer* RECORDS OF *file-name*:** Causes rerun information to be stored on the device defined by implementor name, after the number of records specified have been read or written. *File-name* must be a sequential file opened for output.

+ **RERUN ON *implementor-name* EVERY *integer* CLOCK-UNITS:** Causes rerun information to be stored on the device defined by implementor name after the interval of time specified has passed.

+ **RERUN ON *file-name* EVERY *condition-name*:** Causes rerun information to be stored on the filename specified, which must be a sequential file opened for output, whenever the condition-name specified is true. (*See also* Part V for more information on the PROCEDURE DIVISION.)

✦ **RERUN ON** *implementor-name* **EVERY** *condition-name*:
Causes rerun information to be stored on the device defined by implementor name, whenever the condition-name specified is true. (*See also* Part V for more information on the PROCE-DURE DIVISION.)

The SAME phrase causes the same memory area to be used for two or more files. The SAME phrase can be followed by either the SORT, SORT-MERGE, or RECORD phrases.

The SORT phrase causes the same memory area to be used whenever the SORT or MERGE command is used for the specified files.

The SORT-MERGE phrase is equivalent to the SORT phrase.

If the RECORD phrase is used, the same memory area is used whenever the files specified are read. You can specify more than one SAME phrase, but a filename can't appear in more than one SAME phrase.

The MULTIPLE FILE phrase specifies the location of multiple files contained on a single tape. The position number specified is the file number on the tape. The first file on a tape is always one.

If the POSITION phrase is not specified, the files are assumed to appear on the tape in the order they are specified.

The following code presents a bona-fide example of the I-O-CONTROL SECTION:

```
INPUT-OUTPUT SECTION.
  I-O-CONTROL.
* Store rerun information for file MY-FILE-1
    RERUN ON MY-FILE-1 EVERY END OF REEL
* Use the same area when sorting SORT-FILE-1
* and SORT-FILE-2
    SAME SORT AREA FOR SORT-FILE-1 SORT-FILE-2
* TAPE-FILE-1 and TAPE-FILE-2 are stored on the same
* tape
    MULTIPLE FILE TAPE CONTAINS
      TAPE-FILE-1 POSITION 2
      TAPE-FILE-2 POSITION 6.
```

Part IV

The DATA DIVISION

The DATA DIVISION defines the data used by the program, the hierarchical relationships of the data, and condition names.

The DATA DIVISION is comprised of file, working storage, linkage, communication, and report sections. This part describes the syntax and function of all the paragraphs provided in the DATA DIVISION.

In this part . . .

✔ **Defining communication with systems devices in the** COMMUNICATION SECTION

✔ **Describing the layout and structure of files in the** FILE SECTION

✔ **Communicating between programs using the** LINKAGE SECTION

✔ **Formatting reports using the** REPORT SECTION

The Division's Format

The DATA DIVISION has the following general format:

[**DATA DIVISION**.

[**FILE SECTION**.

    [*file-description-entry*
        {record-description-entry}... or
      sort-merge-file-description-entry
        {record-description-entry}... or
      report-file-description-entry]...]

[**WORKING-STORAGE SECTION**.

    [*77-level-description-entry* or
        record-description-entry]...]

[**LINKAGE SECTION**.

    [*77-level-description-entry* or
        record-description-entry]...]

[**COMMUNICATION SECTION**.

    [*communication-description-entry*
      [*record-description-entry]...]...]*

[**REPORT SECTION**.

    [*report-description-entry*
      {report-group-description-entry}...]...]]

In the ANSI-85 COBOL standard the DATA DIVISION is now optional. In previous standards the DATA DIVISION was a required component.

COMMUNICATION SECTION

The COMMUNICATION SECTION of the DATA DIVISION defines data elements that are used when communicating with system devices. (Communicating with a system device occurs by sending messages through a buffer defined by a communication description entry.)

SEND and RECEIVE commands use Message queues (***see also*** Part VI for more information on these commands).

The format of a communication description entry differs depending on whether the queue is used for input, output, or input and output. The format of these three communication description entries is a follows:

FORMAT 1:

CD *cd-name-1*

FOR [**INITIAL**] **INPUT**

[[[SYMBOLIC **QUEUE** *is data-name-1*]

[SYMBOLIC **SUB-QUEUE-1** IS *data-name-2*]

[SYMBOLIC **SUB-QUEUE-2** IS *data-name-3*]

[SYMBOLIC **SUB-QUEUE-3** IS *data-name-4*]

[**MESSAGE DATE** IS *data-name-5*]

[**MESSAGE TIME** IS *data-name-6*]

[SYMBOLIC **SOURCE** IS *data-name-7*]

[**TEXT LENGTH** IS *data-name-8*]

[**END KEY** IS *data-name-9*]

[**STATUS KEY** IS *data-name-10*]

[**MESSAGE COUNT** IS *data-name-11*]]]

[*data-name-1, data-name-2, data-name-3, data-name-4, data-name-5, data-name-6, data-name-7, data-name-8, data-name-9, data-name-10, data-name-11*]].

FORMAT 2:

CD *cd-name-1 for* **OUTPUT**

[**DESTINATION COUNT** IS *data-name-1*]

[**TEXT LENGTH** IS *data-name-2*]

[**STATUS KEY** IS *data-name-3*]

[**DESTINATION TABLE OCCURS** *integer-1* TIMES
    [**INDEXED** BY {*index-name-1*}...]]

[**ERROR KEY** IS *data-name-4*]

[SYMBOLIC **DESTINATION** IS *data-name-5*].

[*data-name-1, data-name-2, data-name-3, data-name-4, data-name-5*]].

(continued)

(continued)

```
FORMAT 3:

CD cd-name-1

   FOR [INITIAL] I-O

      [[[MESSAGE DATE IS data-name-1]

         [MESSAGE TIME IS data-name-2]

         [SYMBOLIC TERMINAL IS data-name-3]

         [TEXT LENGTH IS data-name-4]

         [END KEY IS data-name-5]

         [STATUS KEY IS data-name-6]]

      [data-name-1, data-name-2, data-name-3, data-name-4,
       data-name-5, data-name-6]].
```

With each type of communication description entry, each data element can be described using its associated phrase (for example, QUEUE, SUB-QUEUE-1, and so on), or data element names can simply be written in order (if you use this form, a name can't be left out).

When names are written in order, the data elements are matched to the order of the phrases in the syntax description. For example, the following two communication description entries are considered to be identical:

```
* This communication description entry...
  CD COMM-1 FOR INPUT
     SYMBOLIC QUEUE IS QUE-1
     SYMBOLIC SUB-QUEUE-1 IS SUB-QUE-1
     SYMBOLIC SUB-QUEUE-2 IS SUB-QUE-2.

* is the same as this communication description entry...
  CD COMM-1 FOR INPUT
     QUE-1, SUB-QUE-1, SUB-QUE-2.
```

In the ANSI-85 COBOL standard, the communication description entry phrases can appear in any order. In previous versions, these entries were required to appear in order.

DESTINATION COUNT

You use the DESTINATION COUNT phrase when defining output type message queues. It defines the data element which contains the number of symbolic destinations that are defined by the message queue.

The destination count is updated whenever a SEND, PURGE, ENABLE OUTPUT, or DISABLE OUTPUT command is executed.

DESTINATION TABLE OCCURS

The DESTINATION TABLE OCCURS phrase defines the size of the output queue message area. If this phrase is not included, the message area is 23 characters long; if it is included, the message area is 13 times the number specified.

END KEY

The END KEY phrase defines a data element that contains a status code that indicates an end message was sent. Use the END KEY phrase when defining input and input-output type message queues. The end key data element is updated after the RECEIVE command is executed. The end key data element holds one character.

The following table identifies the values that can be contained in the end key:

Value	Meaning
0	A RECEIVE MESSAGE or RECEIVE SEGMENT command was executed and an incomplete message or segment was received.
1	An ESI (End Segment Indicator) message was received.
2	An EMI (End Message Indicator) message was received.
3	An EGI (End Group Indicator) message was received.

ERROR KEY

The ERROR KEY phrase identifies the data element that contains the error key for the communication queue. The error key data element is updated after the DISABLE OUTPUT, ENABLE OUTPUT, PURGE, or SEND commands are executed. The error key data element holds one character.

The following table identifies the values that can be contained in the error key:

Value	Meaning
0	No error was detected.
1	The symbolic destination of the queue is unknown.
2	The symbolic destination of the queue is disabled.
4	The symbolic destination of the queue does not have a partial message.

(continued)

Value	Meaning
5	The symbolic destination of the queue has already been enabled or disabled.
6	The output queue is full.
A-Z	These error codes are defined by your specific COBOL compiler or system. Consult your specific compiler documentation for more information on these codes.

INPUT

The INPUT phrase describes a message queue used for input. If you use the optional INITIAL phrase before the INPUT phrase, the contents of the data elements which describe the symbolic queue and sub-queues are set to spaces before any statement in the PROCEDURE DIVISION is executed.

After the first RECEIVE command is executed, the queue and sub-queue data elements contains information about the program which caused the program to be scheduled.

Only one communication description entry can specify the INITIAL phrase, and the INITIAL phrase can't be used in a program where the PROCEDURE DIVISION has a USING clause (*see also* Part V for more information on the USING clause).

I-0

The I-0 phrase describes a message queue used for both input and output. If you use the optional INITIAL phrase before the I-0 phrase, the contents of the data elements which describe the symbolic queue and sub-queues are set to spaces before any statement in the PROCEDURE DIVISION is executed.

After the first RECEIVE command is executed, the queue and sub-queue data elements contain information about the program which caused the program to be scheduled.

Only one communication description entry can specify the INITIAL phrase, and the INITIAL phrase can't be used in a program where the PROCEDURE DIVISION has a USING clause (*see also* Part V for more information on the USING clause).

MESSAGE DATE

The MESSAGE DATE phrase defines a data element that contains the date when a message was sent. The MESSAGE DATE data element can only be used with input and input-output type queues.

The message date data element is six characters long. After a RECEIVE command is executed, the message date data element contains a date of the form YYMMDD (year, month, date).

MESSAGE COUNT

The MESSAGE COUNT phrase defines a data element which contains the number of messages that in a queue or sub-queue whenever the ACCEPT MESSAGE COUNT command is executed.

MESSAGE TIME

The MESSAGE TIME phrase defines a data element that contains the time when a message was sent. The MESSAGE TIME data element can only be used with input and input-output type queues.

The message time data element is eight characters long. After a RECEIVE command is executed, the message time data element contains a time of the form HHMMSSHH (hours, minutes, seconds, hundredths of a second).

OUTPUT

The OUTPUT phrase describes a message queue used for output.

STATUS KEY

The STATUS KEY phrase identifies the data element that contains the status key for the communication queue. The status key data element is updated after the ACCEPT MESSAGE COUNT, DISABLE, ENABLE, PURGE, RECEIVE, or SEND commands are executed. The status key data element holds two characters.

The following table identifies the values that can be contained in the status key:

Value	Meaning
00	No error was detected, and the operation was completed successfully.
10	One or more of the destinations was not available, and the operation was completed for available destinations.
15	The symbolic source or destination queue was enabled or disabled.
20	One or more of the destinations are unknown. The action was completed for the known destinations.
21	The symbolic source was unknown, and the operation was not performed.
30	The destination count was invalid, and the operation was not performed.
40	The password was invalid, and the enable or disable operation was not performed.

(continued)

Value	Meaning
50	The text length is bigger than the length defined by the queue.
60	The portion requested to be sent has a length of zero, and the operation was not performed.
65	The output queue is full, and the operation was not performed.
70	One or more destinations do not have associated portions. The action was completed for destinations with portions.
80	One or more of the conditions (10, 15, or 20) has occurred.
9X	These error codes are defined by your specific COBOL compiler or system. Consult your specific compiler documentation for more information on these codes.

SUB-QUEUE

The SUB-QUEUE phrase defines a data element that contains the contents of a sub-queue to receive messages from. The SUB-QUEUE phrase can only be used with an input type message queue. There can be up to four sub-queues defined for each message queue.

Before the RECEIVE command is executed for the device, the contents of the sub-queue data elements should be set to the symbolic names of the sub-queues data is read from.

SYMBOLIC DESTINATION

The SYMBOLIC DESTINATION phrase defines a data element that contains the name of a queue where a message should be sent. The SYMBOLIC DESTINATION phrase can only be used with an output type message queue.

Before a SEND command is executed for the device, you need to set the contents of the symbolic queue data element to the name of the queue you want to send data to.

SYMBOLIC QUEUE

The SYMBOLIC QUEUE phrase defines a data element that contains the name of the queue to receive messages from. The SYMBOLIC QUEUE phrase can only be used with an input type message queue.

Before a RECEIVE command is executed for a device, you need to set the contents of the symbolic queue data element to the name of the queue you want to read data from.

SYMBOLIC SOURCE

The SYMBOLIC SOURCE phrase defines a data element that contains the source of the message received. The SYMBOLIC SOURCE phrase can only be used when defining input type queues.

The contents of the symbolic source data element is updated after the RECEIVE command is executed. If the message source is not known, the symbolic source data element contains spaces.

SYMBOLIC TERMINAL

The SYMBOLIC TERMINAL phrase defines a data element that contains the symbolic name of the terminal where data is sent to or read from. The SYMBOLIC TERMINAL phrase can only be used when defining input-output type queues.

The symbolic terminal data element contains the name of the terminal where data was read from after the RECEIVE command is executed for the message queue.

The symbolic terminal data element should contain the terminal name to send data to before the SEND command is executed for the message queue.

TEXT LENGTH

The TEXT LENGTH phrase defines a data element which defines the number of characters read from or to be sent to a message queue. The TEXT LENGTH phrase can be used with input, output, and input-output type message queues.

The text length data element is set to the number of characters read after the RECEIVE command is executed for input or input-output type message queues.

The text length data element should be set to the number of characters to send before the SEND command is executed for output type message queues.

FILE SECTION

The FILE SECTION of the DATA DIVISION describes the record structure of the files used by your program. Each file used by the program must have a file control entry, depending on its file type.

While there are five different file types in the FILE SECTION, COBOL only offers three primary methods of file organization (file organization is the way in which data records are stored on a file-storage device):

+ **Sequential file:** In a sequential file, the records are written in a serial order and are read in the same order as written. The serial order doesn't need to be in any particular sequence, such as by account number.

  The CLOSE, OPEN, READ, REWRITE, USE, and WRITE commands can be used with sequential files. The only file access mode that can be used with sequential files is the sequential mode.

+ **Relative file:** A relative file is one in which records are accessed by reference to their relative position in the file. If a file contains 100 records, the first record in the file has a relative key of 1, and the last record has a relative key of 100. A relative file can be read in a random order, by simply using the relative key of each record.

  The CLOSE, DELETE, OPEN, READ, REWRITE, START, USE, and WRITE commands can be used with relative files. Relative files can be accessed in sequential, random, and dynamic mode.

+ **Indexed file:** An indexed file is something of a balance between sequential file organization and relative file organization. It allows sequential storage but also allows the same random accessing or processing of relative files.

  Indexed files utilize an index table that indicates the approximate location for any given record. Unlike relative files, the key to address translation is built-in.

  The CLOSE, DELETE, OPEN, READ, REWRITE, START, USE, and WRITE commands can be used with indexed files. Indexed files can be accessed in sequential, random, and dynamic mode.

Five different file types can be described in the FILE SECTION:

+ **A sequential file:** Records are written in a serial order and are read in the same order as written.

+ **A relative file:** Records are accessed by reference to their relative position in the file.

+ **An indexed file:** Offers something of a balance between sequential file organization and relative file organization. It allows sequential storage but also allows the same random accessing or processing of relative files.

+ **A sort-merge file:** Contains a collection of records to be sorted or merged. A sort-merge file is created when, not surprisingly, you call the SORT or MERGE commands. You use the sort-merge file as a temporary storage area; it can't be accessed outside of the SORT or MERGE commands.

✦ **A report file:** A sequential output file that is defined using the REPORT clause. A report file consists of records that are written by the Report Writer Control System.

Each file type has a different file description format, as the following code shows:

SEQUENTIAL FILE:

> **FD** *file-name-1*
>
> [IS **EXTERNAL**]
>
> [IS **GLOBAL**]
>
>> [**BLOCK** CONTAINS
>>   [*integer-1* **TO**] *integer-2*
>> {**RECORDS** *or* CHARACTERS}]
>>
>> [**RECORD**
>>   {CONTAINS *integer-3* CHARACTERS *or*
>>   IS **VARYING** IN SIZE [[FROM *integer-4*]
>>   [**TO** *integer-5*] CHARACTERS] *or*
>>   [**DEPENDING** ON *data-name-1*] *or*
>>   **CONTAINS** *integer-6* **TO** *integer-7* CHARACTERS}]
>>
>> [**LABEL** {**RECORD** IS *or* **RECORDS** ARE}
>> {**STANDARD** *or* **OMITTED**}]
>>
>> [**VALUE OF** {*implementor-name-1* IS
>>   {*data-name-2 or literal-1*}}...]
>
> [**DATA** {**RECORD** IS *or* **RECORDS** ARE}{*data-name-3*}...]
>
>> [**LINAGE** IS {*data-name-4 or integer-8*}
>>   LINES [WITH **FOOTING** AT
>>   {*data-name-5 or integer-9*}]
>>
>> [LINES AT **TOP**
>>   {*data-name-6 or integer-10*}]
>> [LINES AT **BOTTOM** {*data-name-7 or integer-11*}]]
>
> [**CODE SET** *is alphabet-name-1*].

RELATIVE FILE:

> **FD** *file-name-1*
>   [IS **EXTERNAL**]
>
> [IS **GLOBAL**]
>
>> [**BLOCK** CONTAINS
>>   [*integer-1* **TO**] *integer-2*
>> {**RECORDS** *or* CHARACTERS}]

(continued)

(continued)

```
        [RECORD
          {CONTAINS integer-3 CHARACTERS or
           IS VARYING IN SIZE [[FROM integer-4]
             [TO integer-5] CHARACTERS] or
             [DEPENDING ON data-name-1] or
             CONTAINS integer-6 TO integer-7 CHARACTERS}]

        [LABEL {RECORD IS or RECORDS ARE}
          {STANDARD or OMITTED}]

        [VALUE OF {implementor-name-1 IS
             {data-name-2 or literal-1}}...]

    [DATA {RECORD IS or RECORDS ARE}
             {data-name-3}...].

INDEXED FILE:

        FD file-name-1
             [IS EXTERNAL]

    [IS GLOBAL]

        [BLOCK CONTAINS
          [integer-1 TO] integer-2
   {RECORDS or CHARACTERS}]

        [RECORD
          {CONTAINS integer-3 CHARACTERS or
           IS VARYING IN SIZE [[FROM integer-4]
             [TO integer-5] CHARACTERS] or
             [DEPENDING ON data-name-1] or
             CONTAINS integer-6 TO integer-7 CHARACTERS}]

        [LABEL {RECORD IS or RECORDS ARE}
          {STANDARD or OMITTED}]

        [VALUE OF {implementor-name-1 IS
             {data-name-2 or literal-1}}...]

    [DATA {RECORD IS or RECORDS ARE}
             {data-name-3}...].

SORT-MERGE FILE:

   SD file-name-1

        [RECORD
          {CONTAINS integer-3 CHARACTERS or
           IS VARYING IN SIZE [[FROM integer-4]
             [TO integer-5] CHARACTERS] or
             [DEPENDING ON data-name-1] or
             CONTAINS integer-6 TO integer-7 CHARACTERS}]
```

```
              [DATA {RECORD IS or RECORDS ARE}
                    {data-name-3}...].

      REPORT FILE:

              FD file-name-1
                    [IS EXTERNAL]

      [IS GLOBAL]

              [BLOCK CONTAINS
                    [integer-1 TO] integer-2
              {RECORDS or CHARACTERS}]

              [RECORD
                    {CONTAINS integer-3 CHARACTERS or
                    CONTAINS integer-4 TO integer-5 CHARACTERS}]

              [LABEL {RECORD IS or RECORDS ARE}
                    {STANDARD or OMITTED}]

              [VALUE OF {implementor-name-1 IS
                    {data-name-2 or literal-1}}...]

              [CODE SET IS alphabet-name-1]

              {REPORT IS or REPORTS ARE}{report-name-1}....
```

The data layout of the file follows the file description entry. The data layout describes the order of the fields in each record of a file. A file data description entry has the following three formats:

FORMAT 1:

level-number [*data-name-1* or FILLER]

[REDEFINES *data-name-2*]

[IS EXTERNAL]

[IS GLOBAL]

[{PICTURE or PIC} IS *character-string*]

```
   [[USAGE IS]
   {BINARY or COMPUTATIONAL or COMP or DISPLAY or INDEX
or PACKED-DECIMAL}]
```

[[SIGN IS] {LEADING or TRAILING}[SEPARATE CHARACTER]]

```
   [OCCURS integer-2 TIMES
   [{ASCENDING or DESCENDING}
     KEY IS {data-name-3}...]...
   [INDEXED BY {index-name-1}...]
```

(continued)

(continued)

```
    OCCURS integer-1 TO integer-2 TIMES
      DEPENDING ON data-name-4 or
      [{ASCENDING or DESCENDING}
        KEY IS {data-name-3}...]...
      [INDEXED BY {index-name-1}...]]

[[{SYNCHRONIZED or SYNC}[LEFT or RIGHT]]

[JUSTIFIED or JUST}RIGHT]

[BLANK WHEN ZERO]

[VALUE IS literal-1].

FORMAT 2:

66 data-name-1 RENAMES data-name-2
   [{THROUGH or THRU} data-name-3].

FORMAT 3:

88 condition-name-1 {VALUE IS or VALUES ARE}
   {literal-1 [{THROUGH or THRU} literal-2]}....
```

The file data description Formats 2 and 3 are primarily used in the WORKING STORAGE section of the DATA DIVISION.

BLANK WHEN ZERO

You use the BLANK WHEN ZERO phrase in the file data description entry when defining a record data element. If the data element being defined has the value of zero, whenever it is displayed or printed, blanks are printed instead of a zero or zeroes.

In the ANSI-85 COBOL standard, the BLANK WHEN ZERO phrase can only be used within a file or report description entry, and it can only be used with elementary numeric or numeric edited fields that have a display usage.

The BLANK WHEN ZERO clause can't be used if the PICTURE phrase of the data element contains an asterisk. The BLANK WHEN ZERO clause is also not allowed for items described with the USAGE IS INDEX clause; DBCS items; external or internal floating-point items; items described with USAGE IS POINTER, USAGE IS PROCEDURE-POINTER, or USAGE IS OBJECT REFERENCE.

Stay tuned for an example of the BLANK WHEN ZERO phrase:

```
* Define the MY-FILE-1 record layout
  FD MY-FILE-1.
  01 MY-RECORD.
    05 MY-DATA-1 PIC 9999 BLANK WHEN ZERO.
```

BLOCK

You use the BLOCK phrase in the file description entry section when describing sequential, relative, indexed, and report files. The BLOCK phrase defines the physical record size.

The BLOCK phrase is required unless:

✦ A physical record contains a single logical record (the record defined in the file data description).

✦ The device the file is stored on only has one block size (disk drives typically have a fixed block size).

✦ The number of records stored in a block is defined by the system.

If you use the RECORDS phrase, the block size is defined in terms of the number of records per block. If you use the CHARACTERS phrase, the block size is defined in terms of the number of characters per block.

If only one value is specified, the block size is exactly that many records or characters. If two values are specified, the block size is a size in that range. If the file is external, the block size can only be specified with a single exact value.

An example of the BLOCK phrase follows:

```
* Define the MY-FILE-1 record layout, 20 records per
* block
  FD MY-FILE-1
     BLOCK CONTAINS 20 RECORDS.
  01 MY-RECORD.
     05 MY-DATA-1 PIC 9999 BLANK WHEN ZERO.
```

CODE SET

You use the CODE SET phrase in the file description entry section when describing sequential and report files. If you don't specify the CODE SET phrase, the native character set is used by default. If the CODE SET phrase is specified, all the data in the file must have the display usage specified, and any numeric data items must also have the SIGN IS SEPARATE phrase specified. The alphabet name is specified after the CODE SET phrase is defined in the ENVIRONMENT DIVISION (*see also* Part III for more information on the ENVIRONMENT DIVISION).

Check out this exciting example of the CODE SET phrase:

```
* Define the MY-FILE-1 record layout, using the MY-ALPHA
* character set
```

```
FD MY-FILE-1
   CODE SET IS MY-ALPHA.
01 MY-RECORD.
   05 MY-DATA-1 PIC 9999 BLANK WHEN ZERO.
```

DATA

You use the DATA phrase in the file description entry section to define the records that are associated with a file. Use the DATA phrase when a file contains more than one data type. All data item names listed by this phrase must be defined as an 01 level item.

While this phrase is still part of the ANSI-85 COBOL standard, it is considered obsolete and will be removed from future versions of the language.

The following code presents a great example of the DATA phrase:

```
* Define the MY-FILE-1 record layout
  FD MY-FILE-1
     DATA RECORDS ARE MY-RECORD-1 MY-RECORD-2.
  01 MY-RECORD-1.
     05 MY-DATA-1 PIC 9999 BLANK WHEN ZERO.
     05 MY-DATA-2 PIC XXX.
  01 MY-RECORD-2.
     05 MY-DATA-3 PIC XXXX.
     05 MY-DATA-4 PIC 999 BLANK WHEN ZERO.
```

EXTERNAL

You use the EXTERNAL phrase in the file description entry and file data description to define a data item or record that is available to called programs.

The EXTERNAL phrase is new to the ANSI-85 COBOL standard. It can only be used in the file description entry or at the 01 level of the file data description. If you use the EXTERNAL phrase in a data item description, then the REDEFINES and VALUE clauses can't be used also. If you use the EXTERNAL phrase in the file description entry, then the file and all of its records are defined as external.

An example of the EXTERNAL phrase follows:

```
* Define the MY-FILE-1 record layout as external
  FD MY-FILE-1
     IS EXTERNAL.
  01 MY-RECORD-1.
     05 MY-DATA-1 PIC 9999 BLANK WHEN ZERO.
     05 MY-DATA-2 PIC XXX.
```

FILLER

You use the FILLER phrase in a file data description to define a data item that can't be referenced. A filler data item can have any level number and use any of the data item phrases.

In the ANSI-85 COBOL standard, if a data item is defined without using the FILLER phrase and the data item name is also not specified, then it is assumed to be a filler type data item. A filler data item can also define a group item and use the REDEFINES clause. In previous COBOL versions, this was not allowed.

An example of the FILLER phrase follows:

```
* Define the MY-FILE-1 record layout as external
  FD MY-FILE-1
     IS EXTERNAL.
  01 MY-RECORD-1.
* Define field 1
     05 MY-DATA-1 PIC 9999 BLANK WHEN ZERO.
* Define a filler data item.
     05 FILLER PIC XXXXXXX.
* Define field 2
     05 MY-DATA-2 PIC XXX.
```

GLOBAL

The GLOBAL phrase is new to the ANSI-85 COBOL standard. The GLOBAL phrase defines a file data item, file description, or report as global. The GLOBAL phrase can only be used with 01 level file data items.

If a file is defined as global, the file and all of its records are also defined as global. A global data item or file is available to all nested programs (*see also* Part I for more information about nested programs).

If the GLOBAL phrase defines a data item, the data item can't also use the REDEFINES phrase. If you use the GLOBAL phrase in a file description, it can't also use the SAME RECORD AREA phrase.

Everyone is talking about this example of the GLOBAL phrase:

```
* Define the MY-FILE-1 record layout as global
  FD MY-FILE-1
     IS GLOBAL.
  01 MY-RECORD-1.
     05 MY-DATA-1 PIC 9999 BLANK WHEN ZERO.
     05 MY-DATA-2 PIC XXX.
```

JUSTIFIED (JUST)

You employ the JUSTIFIED or JUST phrase (JUST is shorthand for JUSTIFIED) when defining data items to indicate how alpha-numeric data is stored in a data item.

If the JUSTIFIED clause is not included, the data is left justified. If you use the JUSTIFIED phrase with an OCCURS phrase, it applies to all of the array data elements. When a data item is right justified and the data contains fewer characters than it can hold, it is padded with spaces.

Just look at this example of the JUSTIFIED clause:

```
* Define the MY-FILE-1 record layout
  FD MY-FILE-1
  01 MY-RECORD-1.
     05 MY-DATA-1 PIC XXXX JUSTIFIED RIGHT.
```

LABEL

You use the LABEL phrase in the file description entry to indicate the presence of label records in a file.

In ANSI-85 COBOL this phrase is optional; in previous versions, it was required.

If this phrase is not included, label records are assumed not to exist. If the STANDARD phrase indicates the presence of labels, then they exist in the file.

You need to refer to your COBOL compiler specific documentation to determine how label records are implemented for your system.

An example of the LABEL phrase follows:

```
* Define the MY-FILE-1 record, without label records
  FD MY-FILE-1
     LABEL RECORDS ARE OMITTED.
  01 MY-RECORD-1.
     05 MY-DATA-1 PIC 9999 BLANK WHEN ZERO.
     05 MY-DATA-2 PIC XXX.
```

Level numbers

You employ level numbers when defining data items to indicate a hierarchical relationship that exists between data elements.

Level numbers are the first element used when defining a data item. A level number is a number from 1 to 49, 66, 77, or 88:

+ Level numbers 1 to 49 indicate the relationship among data items. Level number 1 indicates the entire record, which is usually a group item. (A group item is made up of other group and elementary data items that have level numbers greater than itself, and does not actually define storage space for a data item. An elementary data item actually defines storage space.)

✦ Level 77 and 88 data items are defined in the WORKING STORAGE SECTION at the end of this part.

To specify a level number, type the number in Area A and follow the number by a space.

An example of level numbers follows:

```
* Define the MY-FILE-1 record, without label records
  FD MY-FILE-1
     LABEL RECORDS ARE OMITTED.
  01 MY-RECORD-1.
     05 MY-DATA-1 PIC 9999 BLANK WHEN ZERO.
     05 MY-DATA-2.
        10 MY-DATA-3 PIC 9.
        10 MY-DATA-4 PIC 99.
     05 MY-DATA-5 PIC XXX.
```

In this example MY-RECORD-1 is a group item that includes MY-DATA-1, MY-DATA-2, MY-DATA-3, MY-DATA-4, and MY-DATA-5. MY-DATA-2 is another group item that includes MY-DATA-3 and MY-DATA-4. MY-DATA-1, MY-DATA-3, MY-DATA-4, and MY-DATA-5 are elementary data items.

LINAGE

The LINAGE phrase specifies the size of a page when defining a file description entry. The LINAGE phrase determines the number of lines per page, which must be greater than zero.

If you use the FOOTING phrase with the LINAGE phrase, it reserves a number of lines at the bottom of each page for a footer. If the BOTTOM and TOP phrases are used with the LINAGE phrase, they define the number of lines to reserve at the top and bottom of the page for page margins.

The LINAGE values automatically reserve the appropriate number of lines on a page when you use the WRITE command with the ADVANCING PAGE phrase, or a page becomes full.

The following code presents an example of the LINAGE phrase:

```
* Define the MY-FILE-1 record, without label records
  FD MY-FILE-1.
  01 MY-RECORD-1
     LINAGE IS 64 LINES TOP 2 BOTTOM 2.
     05 MY-DATA-1 PIC X(80).
```

OCCURS

You use the OCCURS phrase in the file data description to define tables or arrays. (A table, or array, is a repeating set of data items.) A table may be defined as a fixed size, or a variable size when you use the DEPENDING phrase. When you use the DEPENDING phrase, the value of the data item specified after the phrase determines the table size.

The INDEXED BY phrase is required when defining a table; it specifies the data item that is used as the table index. If the KEY phrase is included, it indicates the data elements used when searching a table.

All file data description phrases can be used when defining a table, even the VALUE phrase, which is new to the ANSI-85 COBOL standard.

The following code presents an example of the OCCURS phrase:

```
* Define a table...
  02 MY-TABLE-1
       OCCURS 20 TIMES
       ASCENDING KEY IS MY-DATA-2
       INDEXED BY N.
    05 MY-DATA-1 PIC 9999 BLANK WHEN ZERO.
    05 MY-DATA-2.
       10 MY-DATA-3 PIC 9.
       10 MY-DATA-4 PIC 99.
    05 MY-DATA-5 PIC XXX.
```

In this example, a table is defined: MY-TABLE-1, which contains the data items, MY-DATA-1, MY-DATA-2, MY-DATA-3, MY-DATA-4, and MY-DATA-5 at each table index. Because the KEY phrase is also specified, the data in MY-DATA-2 is stored in increasing order; this information is used with the SEARCH command. The table index is the data item N.

PICTURE

You use the PICTURE phrase when defining a data element to determine the size and type of data that can be stored in the data item. Each character specified in a PICTURE phrase indicates the data item will occupy a character.

The following table shows you the characters that are allowed when defining the PICTURE phrase type:

Character	Description
9	The 9 character indicates a data item contains numeric data, 0-9.
A	The A character indicates a data item contains alphabetic data, A-Z and a-z.
B	The B character indicates a fixed blank space in a data item. For example, if a data item is defined as ABABAAAAA and the data value JWSMITH is moved into that data item, when it is displayed, J W SMITH will be printed.
P	Use the P character along with the V character to indicate the position of a decimal point when the decimal point is not actually in the number itself. For example, if a data item is defined as 99PPPV and it has a value of 12, its numerical value is equivalent to 12000.
S	The S character indicates a numeric field that is signed. Only one S character should be used in a field, and it must be the leftmost character. For example S9999.
V	The V character indicates the position of an assumed decimal point. Only one V character is permitted per data item. For example, if a data item is defined as 999V99 and its value is 10099, its numerical value equivalent is 100.99.
X	The X character indicates a data item contains alphanumeric data, A-Z, a-z, or 0-9.
Z	The Z character is equivalent to a 9 character, except when the value in that character position is zero, and then a blank is displayed instead.
CR	The CR indicates a CR or credit is displayed if the value is negative. The CR must appear at the end of the picture string. For example, if a data item is defined as 99.99CR, and it has the value -10.50, 10.50CR is displayed when the data item is written.
DB	The DB indicates a DB, or debit, is displayed if the value is negative. The DB must appear at the end of the picture string. For example, if a data item is defined as 99.99DB, and it has the value -10.50, 10.50DB is displayed when the data item is written.
$	The $ character causes a dollar sign to be written when the data item is displayed. The $ character is equivalent to a 9 character. For example, if a data item is defined as $$.99, and it has the value 10.50, $10.50 is displayed when the data item is written.

(continued)

Character	Description
,	The , character causes a comma to be written in a numeric value when the data is displayed. For example, if a data item is defined as $,$$$.99 and it has the value 100099, $1,000.99 is displayed when the data item is written.
.	The . character causes a decimal point to be written in a numeric value when the data is displayed. For example, if a data item is defined as $,$$$.99 and it has the value 100099, $1,000.99 is displayed when the data item is written.
+, -	The + and - characters write the sign of a value when it is displayed. The + and - characters can appear as the first or last item in a picture phrase. For example, if a data item is defined as 999-, and it has the value -10, 10- is displayed when the data item is written.
*	Use the * character as a check protection character. The * is equivalent to the 9 character. For example, if a data item is defined as ****9.99, and it has the value 10.99, ***10.99 is displayed when the data item is written.
0	The 0 character causes zeros to be inserted into a data item. For example, if a data item is defined as 999900, and it has the value 1029, 102900 is displayed when the data item is written.
/	The / character displays a / character when a data item is displayed. For example, if a data item is defined as 99/99/99, and it has the value 121298, 12/12/98 is displayed when the data item is written.

When defining a data item type using PICTURE, a character can simply be repeated a number of times to determine a data size, or a character can be used once followed by a number in parentheses.

The following example illustrates how the PICTURE phrase defines a data item:

```
* Define the MY-FILE-1 record, without label records
  FD MY-FILE-1.
  01 MY-RECORD-1.
* Defines a 4 digit numeric value
    05 MY-DATA-1 PIC 9999.
* Defines a 5 character data value
    05 MY-DATA-3 PIC XXXXX.
* Also defines a 5 character data value
    05 MY-DATA-4 PIC X(5).
* Defines a 6 digit numeric value that contains
* a decimal point
    05 MY-DATA-5 PIC 9999.99.
```

RECORD

You use the RECORD phrase in the file description entry to define the size of a data record. The RECORD phrase indicates how many characters are contained in the data record.

If the VARYING phrase is included, the record size is variable. If the DEPENDING phrase is also included, the record size is determined when the data item specified has a value. When a variable size record is specified with the DEPENDING phrase, the record size is determined whenever a READ or RETURN command is executed and it updates the contents of the data item.

An example of the RECORD phrase follows:

```
* Define the MY-FILE-1 record, without label records
  FD MY-FILE-1
     RECORD IS VARYING 1 TO 10
     DEPENDING ON MY-DATA-1.
  01 MY-RECORD-1.
```

REDEFINES

You employ the REDEFINES phrase in a file data description entry to use the same storage space for multiple descriptions. The REDEFINES phrase can't be used with the OCCURS phrase.

The REDEFINES clause is best understood with an example:

```
02 A.
   05 B PIC XXX.
   05 C PIC X(5).
   05 D PIC XX.
02 W REDEFINES A.
   05 X PIC 999V9.
   05 Y PIC AAA.
   05 Z PIC 999.
```

In this example, the W data item redefines the A data item. The data stored in A and W occupies the same storage space.

SIGN

You use the SIGN phrase in a file data description to define the position and location of a sign. The S in the PICTURE clause makes the data item signed, but it doesn't indicate how or where the sign is stored.

If you use the LEADING phrase, the signed data item is stored in the leading character position. If you use the TRAILING phrase, the signed data item is stored in the trailing character position.

The SEPARATE CHARACTER phrase causes the signed data item to be stored as a separate character. If you use the SIGN phrase with a group data item, it applies to all the elementary data items under it.

Check out this example of the SIGN phrase:

```
* Define the MY-FILE-1 record, without label records
  FD MY-FILE-1.
  01 MY-RECORD-1.
* Defines a 4 digit numeric value, that contains a
* leading sign
    05 MY-DATA-1 PIC S9999
        SIGN IS LEADING SEPARATE CHARACTER.
```

SYNCHRONIZED (SYNC)

You use the SYNCHRONIZED or SYNC (SYNC is just shorthand for SYNCHRONIZED) phrase when defining a data item to make sure that it begins on a natural boundary of computer memory. You need to consult your compiler and system-specific documentation to determine what these boundaries are.

Storing a data item on a natural memory boundary increases the efficiency of access to the data item. You may find it easier for the computer to access data items stored on natural boundaries. While the SYNCHRONIZED clause is never required, it can improve performance on some systems for binary items used in arithmetic.

If you employ the LEFT phrase, the item is stored so the left hand side occurs on a natural memory boundary. If you use the RIGHT phrase, the item is stored so the right hand side occurs on a natural memory boundary. If the LEFT or RIGHT phrase is not specified and you use the SYNCHRONIZED phrase, the VALUE phrase can't be used.

An example of the SYNCHRONIZED phrase follows:

```
* Define the MY-FILE-1 record, without label records
  FD MY-FILE-1.
  01 MY-RECORD-1.
* Defines a 4 digit numeric value, that is synchronized
* right
    05 MY-DATA-1 PIC 9999 SYNCHRONIZED RIGHT.
```

USAGE

You call on the USAGE phrase when defining a data element to specify how it is actually stored. Level 66 or 88 data items can't employ the USAGE phrase.

The following table describes the permissible USAGE types:

Type	Description
BINARY	The data in the item is stored as a binary value, or base 2 value.
PACKED-DECIMAL	The data in the item is stored as a base 10 value. Very useful when storing very large numbers.
COMPUTATIONAL or COMP	The data in the item is stored in a format that is most efficient for processing by the system.
DISPLAY	The data in the item is stored in a standard format — in the same way it would be displayed when written.
INDEX	Use the data item as an index value for a table. The SYNCHRONIZED, JUSTIFIED, PICTURE, VALUE, and BLANK WHEN ZERO phrases can't be used with an index item.

An example of the USAGE phrase follows:

```
* Define the MY-FILE-1 record, without label records
  FD MY-FILE-1.
  01 MY-RECORD-1.
* Defines a 4 digit numeric value, that is synchronized
* and binary
     05 MY-DATA-1 PIC 9999
        SYNCHRONIZED
        USAGE IS BINARY.
```

VALUE

You use the VALUE phrase when describing a data item in the working storage, report, or COMMUNICATION SECTION. The VALUE phrase specifies an initial value of a data item. The initial value must be in the correct form of the data item.

I know that you will really appreciate the following example of the VALUE phrase:

```
* Initialize a dollar amount
  02 A PIC $999.99 VALUE IS "$100.99".

* Initialize a decimal value
  02 A PIC 99V99 VALUE IS 10.99.

* Initialize a group of data items
  02 GROUP VALUE IS "AAA BBB CCC".
* Initialized to AAA
     05 A PIC XXX.
* Initialized to BBB
     05 B PIC XXX.
* Initialized to CCC
     05 C PIC XXX.
```

LINKAGE SECTION

The LINKAGE SECTION is an optional part of the DATA DIVISION. It describes data made available from another program or method when the program is called from another program using the CALL command with the USING phrase (*see also* Part VI for more detailed information on the CALL command).

The data items defined in the LINKAGE SECTION must be level 77 or elementary, data items or a regular record description as described by the file data item description.

When the program is called, the items described in the LINKAGE SECTION contain the values specified by the USING phrase of the CALL command. Each data item defined in the LINKAGE SECTION follows the same rules as the data items defined in the file data item entry section, but a linkage data item must use the PICTURE or USAGE IS INDEX phrase.

REPORT SECTION

The REPORT SECTION defines a report and its associated data items. (A report file is a sequential file that, when written, contains the report described.)

You use a report file with the GENERATE, INITIATE, SUPPRESS, TERMINATE, USE BEFORE REPORTING, and USE AFTER EXCEPTION commands.

Just as each data element of a file must be described by a file item entry, each data item in a report must be described by a report data item entry. A report data item entry can take on any of the following formats:

FORMAT 1:

01 [*data-name-1*]

    [**LINE** NUMBER IS {*integer-1* [ON **NEXT PAGE**] *or*
                    PLUS *integer-2*}]

    [**NEXT GROUP** IS {*integer-3* *or*
                 PLUS *integer-4* *or*
          NEXT PAGE}]

TYPE IS

    {{**REPORT HEADING** *or* **RH**} *or*

    {**PAGE HEADING** *or* **PH**} *or*

{**CONTROL HEADING** or **CH**} {*data-name-2* or **FINAL**} or

{**DETAIL** or **DE**} or

{**CONTROL FOOTING** or **CF**} {*data-name-3* or **FINAL**}

{**PAGE FOOTING** or **PF**} or

{**REPORT FOOTING** or **RF**}}

[[**USAGE** IS] **DISPLAY**].

FORMAT 2:

level-number [*data-name-1*]

   [**LINE** NUMBER IS {*integer-1* [ON **NEXT PAGE**] or
              PLUS *integer-2*}]

     [[**USAGE** IS] **DISPLAY**].

FORMAT 3:

level-number [*data-name-1*]

{**PICTURE** or **PIC**} IS *character-string*

     [[**USAGE** IS] **DISPLAY**]

[[**SIGN** IS]{**LEADING** or **TRAILING**} **SEPARATE** CHARACTER]

[{**JUSTIFIED** or **JUST**} RIGHT]

[**BLANK** WHEN **ZERO**]

   [**LINE** NUMBER IS {*integer-1* [ON **NEXT PAGE**] or
              PLUS *integer-2*}]

[**COLUMN** NUMBER IS *integer-3*]

{**SOURCE** IS *identifier-1* or

VALUE IS *literal-1* or

   {**SUM** {*identifier-2*}...[**UPON** {*data-name-2*}...]}... or
[**RESET** ON {*data-name-3* or **FINAL**}]}

[**GROUP** INDICATE].

BLANK WHEN ZERO

You use the BLANK WHEN ZERO phrase in the file data description
entry when defining a record data element. When the data element
being defined has the value of zero, whenever it is displayed or
printed, blanks are printed instead of a zero or zeroes.

The BLANK WHEN ZERO phrase can only be used within a file or report description entry, and can only be used with elementary numeric or numeric edited fields that have a display usage. This is a new restriction in the ANSI-85 COBOL standard.

BLANK WHEN ZERO can't be used if the PICTURE phrase of the data element contains an asterisk.

An example of the BLANK WHEN ZERO phrase follows:

```
* Define the MY-FILE-1 record layout
  FD MY-FILE-1.
  01 MY-RECORD.
     05 MY-DATA-1 PIC 9999 BLANK WHEN ZERO.
```

GROUP

You use the GROUP phrase when defining a report data item. It indicates that the data item only appears after the first occurrence of the report group after a control break or page advance. The GROUP phrase can only be used with a detail type report data item.

If the GROUP phrase is specified along with the SOURCE or VALUE phrase, the values specified are ignored except when:

✦ The data item first appears in the report.

✦ The data item first appears after every page advance.

✦ The data item first appears after every control break.

JUSTIFIED (JUST)

You use the JUSTIFIED or JUST (JUST is shorthand for JUSTI-FIED) phrase when defining data items to indicate how alphanumeric data is stored in a data item. If the JUSTIFIED clause is not included, the data is left justified. When a data item is right justified and the data contains fewer characters than it is defined to hold, it is padded with spaces.

LINE

You use the LINE phrase when defining a report data item, and it specifies the line number where the data item will appear.

Every report data item must have an associate LINE phrase. If the LINE phrase is not specified for a report data item, it must be specified for the group if the data item is part of one.

The PLUS phrase specifies relative line numbers. When defining data items, items with absolute line numbers must appear first. If you use the NEXT PAGE phrase, it indicates that the data item will appear on a new page indicated by the line number specified.

The maximum line number that can be specified is 999.

PICTURE

You use the PICTURE phrase when defining a data element to determine the size and type of data that can be stored in the data item. Each character specified in a PICTURE phrase indicates the data item will occupy a character. The PICTURE characters are defined in detail in the FILE SECTION, which appears earlier in this part.

SIGN

You use the SIGN phrase in a file data description to define the position and location of a sign. The S in the PICTURE clause makes the data item signed, but it doesn't indicate how or where the sign is stored.

If you use the LEADING phrase, the sign is stored in the leading character position. If you use the TRAILING phrase, the sign is stored in the trailing character position. The SEPARATE CHARAC-TER phrase causes the sign to be stored as a separate character. If you use the SIGN phrase with a group data item, it applies to all the elementary data items under it.

SOURCE

The SOURCE phrase identifies a source data item that should be moved into a printable report data item when the report is generated. The source data item is moved to the printable report data item, just before the report data item is displayed when the report is generated.

SUM

The SUM phrase defines a data item that counts up the value of other data items previously displayed. The sum data item can only appear in a control footing type report data item. A sum data item can be modified while the report is being generated. The sum data item obtains its type and size from the type and size of the data items being summed. If you use the UPON phrase, the data items are added when a GENERATE command for the specified report group is called. If the RESET phrase is specified, the counter is set to zero whenever the control footing is processed.

TYPE

The TYPE phrase specifies the type of the report data item. The following data item types are supported:

✦ If the REPORT HEADING or RH phrase is specified, the data item or the group is a report header. The report header is processed automatically at the start of the report, after the GENERATE command is called.

✦ If the PAGE HEADING or PH phrase is specified, the data item or group is a page header. The page header is processed automatically each time a new page is generated.

✦ If the CONTROL HEADING or CH phrase is specified, the data item or group is a control header. The control heading is processed at the beginning of a control group for the control data name, or if the FINAL phrase is specified when the first GENERATE command is executed for the report.

✦ If the DETAIL or DE phrase is specified, the data item or group is the report detail. One or more detail-type data items or groups must be specified for a report if a GENERATE command is executed for the report.

✦ If the CONTROL FOOTING or CF phrase is specified, the data item or group is a control footer. The control footer is processed at the end of a control group for the control data name, or if the FINAL phrase is specified when the TERMINATE command is executed for the report.

✦ If the PAGE FOOTING or PF phrase is specified, the data item or group is a page footer. The page footer is processed automatically each time a page ends.

✦ If the REPORT FOOTING or RF phrase is specified, the data item or the group is a report footer. The report header is processed automatically at the start of the report after the TERMINATE command is called.

USAGE

You use the USAGE phrase when defining a data element to specify how it is actually stored. The USAGE types are described in detail in the FILE SECTION part earlier in this part.

VALUE

You use the VALUE phrase when describing a data item in the WORKING STORAGE, REPORT, or COMMUNICATION SECTION. The VALUE phrase specifies an initial value of a data item. The initial value must be in the correct form of the data item.

WORKING-STORAGE SECTION

The WORKING STORAGE SECTION defines data items that aren't associated with any files. Data items can be defined using the file data entry description described in the FILE SECTION earlier in this part. Data items can be described using the standard 01 to 49 level numbers. The WORKING STORAGE SECTION also supports 77 and 88 level data items. 77 level data items describe singular data items that don't fit in a hierarchy. 88 level data items describe a condition name (*see also* Part V for more information on conditions).

77 level descriptions

77 level data items describe data items that don't fit into a record hierarchy. These data items are typically data items that are used as counters and for temporary storage. 77 level data items use the same phrases defined for file data item descriptions.

An example of a level 77 data description follows:

```
* Working Storage section
  WORKING STORAGE.
* Define a temporary storage variable
    77 TEMP-DATA PIC X(50).
```

88 level conditions

A condition name is a user-defined word that is associated with one or more values that can be contained in a data item, or is assigned to a status of a user defined switch or device. A condition name is defined as a level 88 data item or in the SPECIAL-NAMES paragraph in the ENVIRONMENT DIVISION.

A level 88 data item is defined using the following format:

```
88 condition-name-1 {VALUE IS or VALUES ARE}
   {literal-1 [{THROUGH or THRU} literal-2]}
```

The VALUE phrase is mandatory when defining a condition name. A condition name can be assigned to a single or consecutive range of data items.

A condition name can only be associated with a consecutive range of values, for example 0 through 10, and not a broken up range, such as 0 through 3 and 5 through 7. You need to define multiple condition names to test for broken up ranges. Multiple condition names can be defined for a data item.

A condition name can't be associated with:

- ✦ A level 66 defined data item
- ✦ An index data item
- ✦ A group item that contains JUSTIFIED or SYNCHRONIZED clauses, or a usage other than DISPLAY
- ✦ A condition name itself

See also Part V for more information on using condition names.

An example of a condition name definition would be as follows:

```
DATA DIVISION.
* Define the data item PRODUCT-NUMBER and associated
* conditions to test for product number ranges.
      02 PRODUCT-NUMBER  PIC 999999.
        88 DUCK-SUPPLIES VALUE IS 0 THRU 111111.
        88 RABIT-SUPPLIES VALUE IS 222222 THRU 333333.
        88 PIG-SUPPLIES VALUE IS 444444 THRU 555555.
        88 COW-SUPPLIES VALUE IS 777777 THRU 999999.
```

Part V

The PROCEDURE DIVISION

The heart of a COBOL program lies in the PROCEDURE DIVISION. The PROCEDURE DIVISION gets all the work done by defining the procedures in a program (hence the name of the division).

Procedures, you remember, are a sequence of instructions or commands that are executed in order. The COBOL programming language calls these commands or instructions *verb*s. Typically, COBOL verbs perform a set of actions using the files and variables defined by the program.

This part reviews how to add comments to your COBOL applications, defines logical conditions which control the flow of your programs, defines the PROCEDURE DIVISION (including declaratives and procedure names), and define basic arithmetic operations. **See also** Part VI for information on all the COBOL verbs.

In this part . . .

- ✔ Using comments to make your COBOL programs easier to understand
- ✔ Controlling the logical flow of your application with conditions
- ✔ Defining the PROCEDURE DIVISION
- ✔ Using arithmetic operations in your COBOL applications

Commenting on Comments

Comments describe the programmer's intent for a section or line of code. A well commented program is worth its weight in gold — at least to the next programmer that needs to muck through existing code.

Without comments, it's not always easy to figure out what the code is doing (although in the following example, choosing more descriptive variable names would help, too!):

```
* Compute Total Payments As The Number of Payments
* Rate Payment Amount
  COMPUTE TP = I * J * K
```

Comments do not effect the actual code. Basically, you tell the compiler not to pay attention to your comments.

To construct a comment, you start in column 7, which is a special area called the *indicator area* (**see also** Part I for more information on the layout of COBOL source programs). By placing an asterisk (*) in the indicator area, you tell the compiler to ignore any text entered on that line.

If a forward slash (/) is placed in column 7, it also indicates that a comment follows — just like an asterisk, but when the source program goes to the printer, a new page command is sent after the comment prints. Again, a line is only interpreted as a comment if it has an asterisk or a forward slash in column 7, otherwise, it's assumed to be code.

The length of a line in your COBOL program depends on the compiler you use. Most COBOL compilers support at least 80 characters.

Don't be afraid to add comments to your COBOL programs — a few well placed comments can really help someone else who's trying to understand your program.

The following example demonstrates the use of a comment (the first line is a comment):

```
* Compute the total of the items
  ADD ITEM-1 ITEM-2 ITEM-3 TO TOTAL
```

Creating Conditions

A *condition* is a logical expression that can be assigned a truth value. Conditions control the executing of your program, based on the value or type of a variable or identifier.

COBOL supports the five different types of conditions described in this section.

Assigning logical operators

You can use logical operators to combine multiple condition expressions. COBOL provides the following three logical operators:

✦ **AND:** The AND operator is logically true if and only if the logical conditions on the left and right hand side of the AND operator are both true. Otherwise, it is false.

✦ **NOT:** The NOT operator is logically true if and only if the condition it comes before is false. The NOT operator effectively changes a condition value to its opposite.

✦ **OR:** The OR operator is logically true if either of the logical conditions on the left and right hand side of the OR operator are true. Otherwise, it is false.

COBOL programs evaluate these expressions from left to right, but parenthesis can override this left-to-right evaluation.

Logical operators use the following format:

```
condition-1 {AND or OR} condition-2
[NOT] condition-1
```

Class conditions

Class conditions determine the type of information stored in a data value. For example, THIS-VALUE IS NUMERIC.

The format of a class condition is:

```
identifier-1 IS [NOT]
  {NUMERIC or
   ALPHABETIC or
   ALPHABETIC-LOWER or
   ALPHABETIC-UPPER or
class-name-1}
```

A class condition is logically true when the contents of the data item being tested is of the type specified. If the optional NOT phrase is included, the class condition is logically true when the data item being tested is NOT of the type specified.

Class conditions are useful when validating input from a file or directly from a user. There are five types of class conditions that can be tested:

✦ ALPHABETIC **class conditions**

✦ ALPHABETIC-LOWER **class conditions**

◆ ALPHABETIC-UPPER **class conditions**

◆ NUMERIC **class conditions**

◆ **User-defined class conditions**

When using the ALPHABETIC class condition, the condition is considered to be true if the data item being tested contains only the characters A through Z (upper-or lower-case) and spaces.

An example of the ALPHABETIC class condition would be the following IF expression:

```
* Move THIS-VALUE to THAT-VALUE if TEST-VALUE contains
* only ALPHABETIC characters
  IF TEST VALUE IS ALPHABETIC THEN
    MOVE THIS-VALUE TO THAT-VALUE
  END-IF
```

The ALPHABETIC-LOWER class condition is new to ANSI-85 COBOL. When using the ALPHABETIC-LOWER class condition, the condition is considered to be true if the data item being tested contains only the lower-case characters A through Z and spaces.

You can see an example of the ALPHABETIC-LOWER class condition in the following IF expression:

```
* Move THIS-VALUE to THAT-VALUE if TEST-VALUE contains
* only lower case ALPHABETIC characters
  IF TEST VALUE IS ALPHABETIC-LOWER THEN
    MOVE THIS-VALUE TO THAT-VALUE
  END-IF
```

The ALPHABETIC-UPPER class condition is new to ANSI-85 COBOL. When using the ALPHABETIC-UPPER class condition, the condition is considered to be true if the data item being tested contains only the upper-case characters A through Z and spaces.

An example of the ALPHABETIC-UPPER class condition would be the following IF expression:

```
* Move THIS-VALUE to THAT-VALUE if TEST-VALUE contains
* only upper case ALPHABETIC characters
  IF TEST VALUE IS ALPHABETIC-UPPER THEN
    MOVE THIS-VALUE TO THAT-VALUE
  END-IF
```

When using the CLASS NAME class condition, the condition is considered to be true if the data item being tested contains only the characters defined by the class name. A class name is defined in the SPECIAL NAMES section of the ENVIRONMENT DIVISION (*see also* Part III for more information on defining class names).

The following example code demonstrates how to define and test for a class name class condition:

```
ENVIRONMENT DIVISION.
* Define the class name binary, for data items that
* only contain ones and zeros.
  SPECIAL NAMES.
        CLASS BINARY IS 0 THROUGH 1.
  .
  .
  .

* Move THIS-VALUE to THAT-VALUE if TEST-VALUE contains
* conforms to the BINARY CLASS
        IF TEST VALUE IS BINARY THEN
           MOVE THIS-VALUE TO THAT-VALUE
        END-IF
```

When defining class names, the values specified must be consecutive characters in the character set currently being used.

When using the NUMERIC class condition, the condition is considered to be true if the data item being tested contains only the characters 0 through 9, and optionally an algebraic sign. An example of the NUMERIC class condition would be the following IF expression:

```
* Move THIS-VALUE to THAT-VALUE if TEST-VALUE contains
* only NUMERIC characters
  IF TEST VALUE IS NUMERIC THEN
     MOVE THIS-VALUE TO THAT-VALUE
  END-IF
```

Condition name conditions

A condition name relates to condition variables (*see also* Part III for more information on defining condition variables). Condition names resemble contained Boolean expressions; by themselves they are true or false. For example, IF THIS-CONDITION THEN ...

A condition name is a user-defined word that is associated with one or more values that can be contained in a data item, or is assigned to a status of a user-defined switch or device.

A condition name is defined as a level 88 data item or in the SPECIAL-NAMES paragraph in the ENVIRONMENT DIVISION (*see also* Part III for more information on the ENVIRONMENT DIVISION).

A level 88 data item is defined using the following format:

```
88 condition-name-1 {VALUE IS or VALUES ARE}
   {literal-1 [{THROUGH or THRU} literal-2]}
```

The VALUE phrase is mandatory when defining a condition name. A condition name can be assigned to a single or consecutive range of data items.

A condition name can only be associated with a consecutive range of values, for example 0 through 10, and not a broken-up range, such as 0 through 3 and 5 through 7. You need to define multiple condition names to test for broken-up ranges. Multiple condition names can be defined for a data item.

A condition name can't be associated with:

+ A level 66 defined data item

+ An index data item

+ A group item that contains JUSTIFIED or SYNCHRONIZED clauses, or a usage other than DISPLAY

+ A condition name itself

For more information on defining data items *see also* Part IV.

The following code provides an example of a condition name definition and test:

```
DATA DIVISION.
* Define the data item PRODUCT-NUMBER and associated
* conditions to test for product number ranges.
        02 PRODUCT-NUMBER  PIC 999999.
            88 DUCK-SUPPLIES VALUE IS 0 TO 111111.
            88 RABIT-SUPPLIES VALUE IS 222222 TO 333333.
            88 PIG-SUPPLIES VALUE IS 444444 TO 555555.
            88 COW-SUPPLIES VALUE IS 777777 TO 999999.
     .
     .
     .

* Move THIS-VALUE to THAT-VALUE if the PRODUCT-NUMBER
* contains a DUCK-SUPPLIES product number
        IF DUCK-SUPPLIES THEN
           MOVE THIS-VALUE TO THAT-VALUE
        END-IF
```

In this example, the range of values covered by condition names is incomplete. If the product number is in the ranges 111112 to 222221 or 555556 to 777776, all of the condition names will be false.

A relationship test can always be used instead of a condition name, but defining and using condition names can make your code easier to understand. If you need to change the range of a condition later, you can easily do it everywhere by simply changing the condition name definition instead of searching for values throughout your entire program.

Relation conditions

A relation condition determines whether or not a relationship exists between two operands. For example, THIS-VALUE > THAT-VALUE.

The format of a relationship condition is:

```
{identifier-1 or
 literal-1 or
 arithmetic-expression-1 or
 index-name-1}
{IS [NOT] GREATER THAN or
 IS [NOT] > or
 IS [NOT] LESS THAN or
 IS [NOT] < or
 IS [NOT] EQUAL TO or
 IS [NOT] = or
 IS GREATER THAN OR EQUAL TO or
 IS >= or
 IS LESS THAN OR EQUAL TO or
 IS <=}
{identifier-2 or
 literal-2 or
 arithmetic-expression-2 or
index-name-2}
```

Both sides of a relation expression can't be literals. There must be at least one variable in the relation expression.

The expression is logically true if the specified relationship holds between both sides of the relation expression. Otherwise, the expression is false.

If both sides of the relation expression are numeric, a numeric comparison is made. If either side of the expression in non-numeric, then a non-numeric comparison takes place.

When making a non-numeric comparison, if one side is shorter than another, then the shorter side is treated as if it were extended to the same size as the longer operator. When making a non-numeric values, values are compared according to the collating sequence, the character ordering, specified in the ENVIRONMENT DIVISION.

There are five types of relational comparisons that can be made:

✦ EQUAL TO

✦ GREATER THAN

✦ GREATER THAN OR EQUAL TO

✦ LESS THAN

✦ LESS THAN OR EQUAL TO

When using the EQUAL TO (=) relational operator, the relationship is considered to be true when the value on the left hand side is equal to the right hand side. Otherwise the relationship is false. The EQUAL TO phrase or the = symbol can be used interchangeably.

An example of the EQUAL TO or = phrase would be the following IF expression:

```
* Increment COUNTER If THIS-VALUE = THAT-VALUE
  IF THIS-VALUE = THAT-VALUE THEN
    ADD 1 TO COUNTER
  END-IF
```

When using the GREATER THAN (>) relational operator, the relationship is considered to be true when the value on the left hand side is greater than the right hand side. Otherwise, the relationship is false. The GREATER THAN phrase or the > symbol can be used interchangeably.

An example of the GREATER THAN phrase would be the following IF expression:

```
* Increment COUNTER If THIS-VALUE > THAT-VALUE
  IF THIS-VALUE GREATER THAN THAT-VALUE THEN
    ADD 1 TO COUNTER
  END-IF
```

The GREATER THAN OR EQUAL TO (>=) relational operator is new to ANSI-85 COBOL. In previous versions of COBOL, this relation had to be checked with two separate conditions — a check for greater than and a check for equality.

When using the GREATER THAN OR EQUAL TO or >= relational operator, the relationship is considered to be true when the value on the left hand side is greater than or equal to the right hand side. Otherwise the relationship is false. The GREATER THAN OR EQUAL TO phrase or the >= symbol can be used interchangeably.

An example of the GREATER THAN OR EQUAL phrase would be the following IF expression:

```
* Increment COUNTER If THIS-VALUE >= THAT-VALUE
  IF THIS-VALUE GREATER THAN OR EQUAL THAT-VALUE THEN
    ADD 1 TO COUNTER
  END-IF
```

When using the LESS THAN (<) relational operator, the relationship is considered to be true when the value on the left hand side is less than the right hand side. Otherwise, the relationship is false. The LESS THAN phrase or the < symbol can be used interchangeably.

An example of the LESS THAN phrase would be the following IF expression:

```
* Increment COUNTER If THIS-VALUE < THAT-VALUE
  IF THIS-VALUE LESS THAN THAT-VALUE THEN
     ADD 1 TO COUNTER
  END-IF
```

The LESS THAN OR EQUAL TO (<=) relational operator is new to ANSI-85 COBOL. In previous versions of COBOL, this relation had to be checked with two separate conditions — a check for less than and a check for equality.

When using the LESS THAN OR EQUAL TO or <= relational operator, the relationship is considered to be true when the value on the left hand side is less than or equal to the right hand side. Otherwise, the relationship is false. The LESS THAN OR EQUAL TO phrase or the <= symbol can be used interchangeably.

An example of the LESS THAN OR EQUAL phrase would be the following IF expression:

```
* Increment COUNTER If THIS-VALUE >= THAT-VALUE
  IF THIS-VALUE GREATER THAN OR EQUAL THAT-VALUE THEN
     ADD 1 TO COUNTER
  END-IF
```

Sign conditions

You use the sign condition to determine the algebraic result of an expression, either a data item or arithmetic expression. For example, IF THIS-VALUE IS POSITIVE.

The format of the sign condition is:

```
arithmetic-expression-1 IS [NOT]
   {POSITIVE or
    NEGATIVE or
 ZERO}
```

A sign condition is logically true when the contents of the data item being tested are the same as the sign type specified. If the optional NOT phrase is included, the class condition is logically true when the data item being tested is not the same as the sign type specified.

There are three types of sign conditions that can be tested: NEGATIVE, POSITIVE, and ZERO.

A sign condition test can only be performed on numeric data items or arithmetic expressions.

When using the NEGATIVE sign condition, the condition is considered to be true if the data item being tested is less than zero.

An example of the NEGATIVE sign condition would be the following IF expression:

```
* Increment COUNTER If THIS-VALUE Is NEGATIVE
  IF THIS-VALUE IS NEGATIVE THEN
     ADD 1 TO COUNTER
  END-IF
```

When using the POSITIVE sign condition, the condition is considered to be true if the data item being tested is greater than zero.

An example of the POSITIVE sign condition would be the following IF expression:

```
* Increment COUNTER If THIS-VALUE + 100 Is POSITIVE
  IF THIS-VALUE + 100 IS POSITIVE THEN
     ADD 1 TO COUNTER
  END-IF
```

When using the ZERO sign condition, the condition is considered to be true if the data item being tested is equal to zero.

An example of the ZERO sign condition would be the following IF expression:

```
* Increment COUNTER If THIS-VALUE Is NOT ZERO
  IF THIS-VALUE IS NOT ZERO THEN
     ADD 1 TO COUNTER
  END-IF
```

Switch status conditions

Switch status conditions determine whether a switch is on or off. Switches are defined in the SPECIAL NAMES section of the ENVIRONMENT DIVISION (***see also*** Part III for more information on defining switches in the ENVIRONMENT DIVISION).

Defining the PROCEDURE DIVISION

As you can tell from its name, the PROCEDURE DIVISION is where procedures are defined. *Procedures* are a sequence of instructions or commands that are executed in order.

The PROCEDURE DIVISION is the last division in the source program, and in ANSI-85 COBOL it is now an optional division. Like all of the other divisions in a COBOL program, the PROCEDURE DIVISION begins with the PROCEDURE DIVISION header.

There are two formats for the PROCEDURE DIVISION header:

FORMAT 1:

[PROCEDURE DIVISION [USING {data-name-1}...].

[DECLARATIVES.

  {section-name SECTION [segment-number].

  USE statement.

  [paragraph-name.

  [sentence]...]...}...

END DECLARATIVES.]

  {section-name SECTION [segment-number].

  [paragraph-name.

  [sentence]...]...}....]

FORMAT 2:

[PROCEDURE DIVISION [USING {data-name-1}...].

  {paragraph-name.

  [sentence]...}...]

You use Format 1 when declaratives are defined. (_Declaratives_ are a group of one or more special purpose procedures.)

The USE FOR DEBUGGING and USE AFTER EXCEPTION commands can be defined in the declaratives sections (**_see also_** Part IX for more information on these debugging directives).

You employ the USING phrase to pass data items between programs when using the CALL command.

Once the PROCEDURE DIVISION header is defined, paragraph (or procedure) names and commands can follow. The commands immediately following the procedure name are executed first.

An example of a basic PROCEDURE DIVISION header is:

```
* Define The Procedure Division
  PROCEDURE DIVISION.
* ************************
* Start the Main Program
* ************************
  100-MAIN.
* Define the Main Program Here
```

Declaratives

The declarative section defines a group of one or more special purpose procedures. These procedures are primarily used with the USE FOR DEBUGGING, USE AFTER EXCEPTION, and USE

BEFORE REPORTING commands. (For more information on the USE FOR DEBUGGING and USE AFTER EXCEPTION commands, **see also** Part IX. For more information on the reporting directives, **see also** Part IV.) These commands define procedure handlers used for debugging and reporting.

The declaratives section begins with the DECLARATIVES keyword and ends with the END DECLARATIVES keywords.

The following example illustrates the definition of an input file exception handler (the exception handler needs to be defined in the declaratives section of the PROCEDURE DIVISION):

```
* Define The Procedure Division
  PROCEDURE DIVISION USING DATA-1 DATA-2 DATA-3.
  DECLARATIVES.
     USE AFTER EXCEPTION ON INPUT.
     INPUT-FILE-HANDLER.
* Define Input exception file handler routine here
  END DECLARATIVES.
* ************************
* Start the Main Program
* ************************
  100-MAIN.
* Define the Main Program Here
```

Procedure names

Procedure names (sometimes referred to as paragraph names) are user-defined words that identify a sequence of commands.

A procedure name can consist only of digits. Procedure names are identical if, and only if, they contain the same number of characters in the same positions.

Examples of valid procedure names are 100-MAIN, 100, FILE-HANDLER. (The procedure names 001-MAIN and 1-MAIN are not the same — because procedure names are treated as character strings, 001 is not treated as a number, but rather as a string of characters.)

A paragraph or procedure name must begin in Area A and be followed by a period. The first command in a paragraph or procedure can begin on the same line or in Area B of the following line. (**See also** Part I for more information on Area A, B, and the indicator area.)

You use the PERFORM command to call a paragraph or procedure name (**see also** Part VI for more information on the PERFORM command).

USING

The USING phrase passes data items between programs when using the CALL command. (*See also* Part VI for more information on CALL.)

Generally, most COBOL compilers place no limit on the number of parameters that can be passed with the USING phrase. The data items defined by the USING phrase must be defined in the DATA DIVISION of the program.

The following example defines a PROCEDURE DIVISION header which accepts three data items when called:

```
* Define The Procedure Division
  PROCEDURE DIVISION USING DATA-1 DATA-2 DATA-3.
* ***********************
* Start the Main Program
* ***********************
  100-MAIN.
* Define the Main Program Here
```

Performing Arithmetic

COBOL provides a set of basic arithmetic operators, all of which can have one or two operands.

The following table summarizes the COBOL arithmetic operators that take two operands:

Operator	Description	Example
+	Addition	1 + 1, results in 2
−	Subtraction	10 − 5, results in 5
*	Multiplication	5 * 5, results in 25
/	Division	10 / 5, results in 2
**	Exponentation	2 ** 3, results in 8

The + and − operators are also single operand operators, and they must come before a value. For example, −5 or +1234.

Part VI

COBOL Verbs

Just as verbs describe the action in a sentence, COBOL verbs describe the action of your program. They define the step by step actions your COBOL programs take, from verbs which open, read, and process files, to verbs which add, divide, and multiply identifier values.

This part provides a reference for each of the COBOL verbs described by ANSI-85 COBOL. Your specific compiler may provide other non-standard verbs that are specific to your platform. You must consult your compiler documentation for more information if you don't find a verb you're looking for in this part.

In this part . . .

✓ Understanding the syntax and logic of COBOL verbs

✓ Enjoying a complete reference to all the standard verbs supported in COBOL

ACCEPT

The ACCEPT command stores data from a terminal, hardware device, or date information into a user-defined data item.

The ACCEPT command has the following three formats:

FORMAT 1:

ACCEPT *identifier-1* [FROM *mnemonic-name-1*].

FORMAT 2:

ACCEPT *identifier-2* FROM
  {DATE *or* DAY *or* DAY-OF-WEEK *or* TIME}.

FORMAT 3:

ACCEPT *cd-name-1* MESSAGE COUNT.

When using Format 1 of the ACCEPT command, keep the following points in mind:

✦ The ACCEPT statement reads data from either the CONSOLE (system logical console) or SYSIN (system logical input unit) devices and then stores it in identifier-1. The read data is not edited or checked for errors.

✦ If the FROM phrase is omitted, the mnemonic-name SYSIN is assumed.

✦ If the mnemonic-name corresponding to SYSIN is specified as mnemonic-name-1, records are continuously read and stored in order for each identifier specified. The ACCEPT statement continues reading data until all data items specified have received data, or until there are no longer any records to read.

When using Format 2 of the ACCEPT command, keep the following points in mind:

✦ DATE is treated as an unsigned six-digit decimal integer item. If you use DATE, the last two digits of the year, the month, then the day are copied into identifier-2 (a total of six digits). For example, if the date is April 12, 1995, the value copied to identifier-2 is 950412.

✦ DAY is treated as an unsigned five-digit decimal integer item. If you use DAY, then the last two digits of a year, followed by the total number of the days since January 1 are copied into identifier-2. For example, if the date is January 1, 1999, the value copied to identifier-2 is 99001.

✦ TIME is treated as an unsigned eight-digit decimal integer item. If you use TIME, then the current hour in 24-hour format, followed by the current minute, followed by the current second, followed by current hundredths of a second are copied to identifer-2. For example, if the time is exactly 4:48 p.m., the value copied to identifier-2 is 16480000.

✦ DAY-OF-WEEK is treated as an unsigned one-digit decimal integer item. If you use DAY-OF-WEEK, one digit indicating the current day of the week is copied into identifier-2. If the day of the week is Monday, 1 is copied; if it is Tuesday, 2 is copied; if it is Sunday, 7 is copied.

When using Format 1 and Format 2 of the ACCEPT statement, identifier-1 and identifer-2 must be an alphabetic item, alphanumeric data item, zoned decimal item, packed decimal item, binary item, external Boolean item, or fixed-length group item.

When using Format 3 of the ACCEPT command, the message count item for the communications device specified is read into the communication description entry for device cd-name-1. (*See also* Part III for more information on defining a communication entry.)

The following code shows you an example of the ACCEPT command which stores the current DATE in the TODAY data item:

```
* Store today's date in the NOW data item
  ACCEPT NOW FROM TODAY.
```

ADD

The ADD command sums one or more data items and stores the result in another data item.

The ADD command has the following three formats:

FORMAT 1:

```
ADD {identifier-1 or literal-1}...
   TO {identifier-2 [ROUNDED]}...
[ON SIZE ERROR imperative-statement-1]
[NOT ON SIZE ERROR imperative-statement-2]
[END-ADD].
```

FORMAT 2:

```
ADD {identifier-1 or literal-1}...
   TO {identifier-2 or literal-2}
GIVING {identifier-3 [ROUNDED]}...
[ON SIZE ERROR imperative-statement-1]
[NOT ON SIZE ERROR imperative-statement-2]
[END-ADD].
```

(continued)

(continued)
FORMAT 3:

```
ADD {CORRESPONDING or CORR}
    identifier-1 TO identifier-2 [ROUNDED]
[ON SIZE ERROR imperative-statement-1]
[NOT ON SIZE ERROR imperative-statement-2]
[END-ADD].
```

When using Format 1 of the ADD command, the numeric value in identifier-1 or literal-1 is added to the value stored in identifier-2, and the result is stored in identifier-2. If more than one identifier or literal is specified before the TO phrase, these values are summed and then added to identifier-2.

Format 3 of the ADD command includes the CORRESPONDING phrase, but is otherwise the same as Format 1 (*see also* "Phrases" in this part for more information on CORRESPONDING phrases).

The following example of the ADD command illustrates how you can employ Format 1. If DATA-1 has the value 100, then:

```
* Stores DATA-1 + 5, or 100 + 5, or 105 in DATA-1
  ADD 5 TO DATA-1.
* Stores DATA-1 + (5 + 5), or 105 + 10, or 115, in DATA-1
  ADD 5 5 TO DATA-1.
```

Format 2 of the ADD command functions in the same way as Format 1, except the result is stored in the data item specified after the GIVING phrase.

The following example of the ADD command illustrates how you can put Format 2 to work for you. If DATA-1 has the value 100, then:

```
* Stores the value DATA-1 + 5, or 100 + 5, or 105,
* into DATA-2
  ADD 5 TO DATA-1 GIVING DATA-2.
```

See also "Phrases" in this part for more information about the ROUNDED, ON SIZE ERROR, and CORRESPONDING phrases.

ALTER

The ALTER command changes the destination of a GO TO statement from one procedure name to another.

The ALTER command has the following format:

```
ALTER {procedure-name-1 TO
    [PROCEED TO] procedure-name-2}...
```

The ALTER command is still part of the ANSI-85 COBOL standard, but it is scheduled to be removed from future versions of COBOL. You should try to avoid using this command if at all possible.

Check out the following example of ACCEPT, which changes the destination of the GO TO statement written in the SPACE-PROCE-DURE to the TIME-PROCEDURE:

```
* Time to ALTER SPACE and TIME...
  ALTER SPACE-PROCEDURE TO TIME-PROCEDURE.
```

The ALTER statement encourages the use of unstructured programming practices. You should avoid using the ALTER command if possible. The EVALUATE command can be used to provide the same function, and helps to assure that your program remains well structured.

CALL

The CALL command transfers control from one program to another. The CALL command has the following two formats:

FORMAT 1:

```
CALL {identifier-1 or literal-1 or procedure-pointer-1}
   [USING {[BY REFERENCE] {identifier-2}... or
            BY CONTENT {identifier-2}...}...]
[ON OVERFLOW imperative-statement-1]
[END-CALL].
```

FORMAT 2:

```
CALL {identifier-1 or literal-1 or procedure-pointer-1}
   [USING {[BY REFERENCE] {identifier-2}... or
            BY CONTENT {identifier-2}...}...]
[ON EXCEPTION imperative-statement-1]
[NOT ON EXCEPTION imperative-statement-2]
[END-CALL].
```

Keep the following points in mind when using the CALL command:

✦ Identifier-1 or literal-1 must be an alphanumeric data item which identifies the name of the program to be called.

✦ Procedure-pointer-1 must be defined with the USAGE IS PROCEDURE-POINTER phrase, and must be set to a valid program entry point; otherwise, the results of the CALL statement are undefined.

✦ The USING phrase passes values to the program being called. If you use the BY REFERENCE phrase and the value of the data item specified is changed in the program being called, that change is reflected in the calling program.

When you use the BY CONTENT phrase, if the value of the data item specified is changed in the program being called, that change is not reflected in the calling program.

If the BY REFERENCE phrase is either specified or implied for a parameter, the corresponding data item in the calling program occupies the same storage area as the data item in the called program.

✦ The OVERFLOW phrase is only included to maintain compatibility with ANSI-74 COBOL. If an overflow condition occurs when the CALL command is executed, the command following the OVERFLOW phrase is executed.

✦ If the ON EXCEPTION phrase is included, the command following the ON EXCEPTION phrase is executed if an error occurs when the CALL command is executed. If the NOT ON EXCEPTION phrase is included, the command following the NOT ON EXCEPTION phrase is executed if an error doesn't occur when the CALL command is executed.

Can you handle this example of the CALL command? I wonder:

```
* Call the OTHER-PROGRAM passing the parameter DATA-1 by
* reference and DATA-2 by value
 CALL "OTHER-PROGRAM"
    USING DATA-1 BY REFERENCE
          DATA-2 BY CONTENT
 END-CALL.
```

CANCEL

The CANCEL command ensures that the next time a program is called using the CALL command, it is returned to its initial state. The CANCEL command has the following format:

CANCEL {identifier-1 *or* literal-1}...

When using the CANCEL command, the contents of the data item identifier-1 or literal-1 must be the names of programs that can be called from the program. (*See also* Part I for more information about the CALL command and nested programs.)

The following code shows an example of the CANCEL command:

```
* Cancel The CALL to The Program RunBabyRun
 CANCEL "RunBabyRun".
```

CLOSE

The CLOSE command finishes the processing of a file. If the file is stored on a tape (pretty much an unlikely event these days) the close command can also rewind and lock the tape. The CLOSE command has the following two formats:

FORMAT 1:

CLOSE

   {file-name-1

      [{REEL *or* UNIT} [FOR REMOVAL] *or*

      WITH {NO REWIND *or* LOCK}]}...

FORMAT 2:

CLOSE {file-name-1 [WITH LOCK]}...

When using Format 1 of the CLOSE command, keep the following points in mind:

+ If you use the WITH NO REWIND phrase, file-name-1 must be a sequential file.

+ If you use the REEL or UNIT phrase, file-name-1 must be a sequential file or a print file that was opened without the FORMAT clause.

When using Format 2 of the CLOSE command, remember the following points:

+ If you use the LOCK phrase, the file is closed and reopened for exclusive access.

+ Don't forget to consume a salty snack to provide a little variety in your life.

With both formats of the CLOSE command:

+ After the CLOSE command is executed, the input-output status for file-name-1 is updated. Any records which have not yet been written are written to the file, and it is closed.

+ The file, file-name-1, must be already be opened before the CLOSE command is called.

+ If you specify more than one file name with the CLOSE command, it's just like using multiple CLOSE commands for each file.

Check out the following example of the CLOSE command which closes the FILE-OF-DOOM:

```
* Close the File of Doom
  CLOSE FILE-OF-DOOM.
```

COMPUTE

The COMPUTE command stores the result of an arithmetic expression into a data item. The COMPUTE statement has the following format:

```
COMPUTE {identifier-1 [ROUNDED]}...
  = arithmetic-expression-1
[ON SIZE ERROR imperative-statement-1]
[NOT ON SIZE ERROR imperative-statement-2]
[END-COMPUTE].
```

While the ADD, MULTIPLY, and DIVIDE commands allow you to perform a single operation, the COMPUTE command allows you to use the arithmetic operators to compute the result of a complex mathematical express. (**See also** Part II for more information on the COBOL arithmetic operators.)

The COMPUTE command stores the result of the arithmetic expression in the data item identifier-1. Parentheses can be used to control the order of evaluation in the arithmetic expression, which is otherwise left to right.

An example of the COMPUTE command follows:

```
* You're a computer, so compute already...
  COMPUTE DATA-1 = 100 + 50.
  COMPUTE DATA-2 = (DATA-3 + 50) / (DATA-4 * 67).
```

CONTINUE

The CONTINUE command simply does nothing — yes that's right — nothing. It has the following format:

```
CONTINUE.
```

Why would you want to have a statement that does nothing? Well, you may need a statement that's just a place holder — for example, the common exit point of a series of routines. The CONTINUE statement allows you to specify a non-operation statement. CONTINUE indicates that no executable instruction is present.

DELETE

The DELETE command removes a record from a file and has the following format:

```
DELETE file-name-1 RECORD
  [INVALID KEY imperative-statement-1]
  [NOT INVALID KEY imperative-statement-2]
  [END-DELETE].
```

When using the DELETE command, keep the following points in mind:

+ The READ command must be executed for the file before execution of the DELETE command. If the READ command is executed successfully, execution of the DELETE command removes the record read by the READ statement from a file.

+ The INVALID KEY and NOT INVALID KEY statements are used with indexed and relative files. The statements specified are executed based on keys used in the last READ command.

+ If file-name-1 is a sequential file, the INVALID KEY or NOT INVALID KEY phrases can't be used.

+ If you attempt to delete a record that is locked, the DELETE command will fail. The I-O status will contain the error encountered (***see also*** Part III for more information on using I-O status and the codes returned).

+ After the DELETE command has been executed, the record removed from the file can no longer be READ.

+ If the DELETE command is executed successfully, the current file position indicator is not changed.

And now, for your viewing pleasure, here's an example of the DELETE command which removes the current record from the BLAST-OFF-FILE:

```
* Delete the current record, call UH-OH-WRONG-ONE if
* the key is invalid
  DELETE BLAST-OFF-FILE
    INVALID KEY PERFORM UH-OH-WRONG-ONE
  END-DELETE.
```

The BLAST-OFF-FILE must be opened in input-output mode, be a relative or index type file, and be defined with an FD entry in the DATA DIVISION. (***See also*** Part IV for more information on the DATA DIVISION.)

DISABLE

The DISABLE command stops transfers of information between input queues and destinations. The DISABLE command has the following format:

```
DISABLE
    {INPUT [TERMINAL] or I-O TERMINAL or OUTPUT} cd-name-1
    [WITH KEY {identifier-1 or literal-1}].
```

When using the DISABLE command, watch out for the following items:

+ If you use the INPUT phrase, cd-name-1 must refer to an input communication device. If the TERMINAL phrase is not also used, all sub-queues associated with the device are also closed.

+ If you use the I-O TERMINAL phrase, cd-name-1 must refer to an input-output communication device.

+ If you use the OUTPUT phrase, cd-name-1 must refer to an output communication device.

+ To avoid turning off devices a program doesn't have access to, use the WITH KEY phrase. If the key contained in the literal or data item matches the system password for the device, then the queue is disabled. Consult your system documentation for further information. (While this phrase is still part of ANSI-85 COBOL, it is scheduled to be removed from future versions. You should avoid using the WITH KEY phrase if possible.)

In the following code, I show you an example of the DISABLE command which disables the output device MY-DEVICE:

```
* Disable MY-DEVICE
  DISABLE OUTPUT MY-DEVICE.
```

DISPLAY

The DISPLAY command displays the contents of a data item on a terminal or hardware device. The DISPLAY command has the following format:

```
DISPLAY {identifier-1 or literal-1}...
    [UPON mnemonic-name-1] [WITH NO ADVANCING].
```

When using the DISPLAY command, keep the following points in mind:

+ If identifier-1 or literal-1 is an integer, it must be an unsigned integer.

♦ If you use mnemonic-name-1, it must be associated with one of the following output devices: CONSOLE, SYSOUT, SYSERR, or SYSPUNCH.

♦ If the UPON phrase is not used, the SYSOUT device is assumed.

♦ If the WITH NO ADVANCING phrase is not used, after the last data item has been transferred to the hardware device, a line feed is performed. If the WITH NO ADVANCING phrase is written, after the last data item has been displayed, a line feed is not performed.

An example of the DISPLAY command that does the old "Hello World!" routine follows:

```
* Be nice and say hello now...
DISPLAY "Hello World!".
```

DIVIDE

The DIVIDE command divides one data item into another data item and stores the result or the quotient and remainder into other data items. The DIVIDE statement has the following five formats:

FORMAT 1:

```
DIVIDE {identifier-1 or literal-1}
    INTO {identifier-2 [ROUNDED]}...
    [ON SIZE ERROR imperative-statement-1]
[NOT ON SIZE ERROR imperative-statement-2]
[END-DIVIDE].
```

FORMAT 2:

```
DIVIDE {identifier-1 or literal-1}
    INTO {identifier-2 or literal-2}
GIVING {identifier-3 [ROUNDED]}...
    [ON SIZE ERROR imperative-statement-1]
[NOT ON SIZE ERROR imperative-statement-2]
[END-DIVIDE].
```

FORMAT 3:

```
DIVIDE {identifier-1 or literal-1}
    BY {identifier-2 or literal-2}
GIVING {identifier-3 [ROUNDED]}...
    [ON SIZE ERROR imperative-statement-1]
[NOT ON SIZE ERROR imperative-statement-2]
[END-DIVIDE].
```

(continued)

(continued)
```
FORMAT 4:

DIVIDE {identifier-1 or literal-1}
  INTO {identifier-2 or literal-2}
  GIVING identifier-3 [ROUNDED]
REMAINDER identifier-4
  [ON SIZE ERROR imperative-statement-1]
[NOT ON SIZE ERROR imperative-statement-2]
[END-DIVIDE].

FORMAT 5:

DIVIDE {identifier-1 or literal-1}
  BY {identifier-2 or literal-2}
GIVING {identifier-3 [ROUNDED]}...
REMAINDER identifier-4
  [ON SIZE ERROR imperative-statement-1]
[NOT ON SIZE ERROR imperative-statement-2]
[END-DIVIDE].
```

When using Format 1 of the DIVIDE command, the numeric value in identifier-1 or literal-1 is divided into the value stored in identifier-2, and the result is stored in identifier-2.

For example, if DATA-1 has the value 100, then:

```
* Stores DATA-1 / 5, or 100 / 5, or 20 in DATA-1
  DIVIDE 5 INTO DATA-1.
```

Format 2 of the DIVIDE command is the same as Format 1, except that the result is stored in identifier-3. In the following DIVIDE command, the DATA-1 is divided by DATA-2, and the result is stored in DATA-3:

```
* Stores DATA-1 / DATA-2 in DATA-3
  DIVIDE DATA-2 INTO DATA-1 GIVING DATA-2.
```

Format 5 of the DIVIDE command is the same as Format 1, except if division produces a remainder, it is stored in identifier-4. Not all division works out evenly, for example, 5 divided by 2 results in 2.5 (in this example 5 is the dividend and 2 is the divisor). The result of a division can also be broken down into a quotient and a remainder. The remainder of this division is computed by multiplying the fraction portion of the result, in this case .5, by the divisor, in this case 2. This results in a remainder of 1, the result of .5 * 2.

In the following example, I show you a DIVIDE statement which produces a remainder. Assume DATA-3 is an integer data item that has the value 5:

```
* Stores DATA-3 / 2, or 5 / 2, or 2 in DATA-3 and
* stores a remainder of 1 in DATA-4
  DIVIDE 2 INTO DATA-3 REMAINDER DATA-4.
```

Format 3 of the DIVIDE command functions in the same way as Format 1, except the result is stored in the data item specified after the GIVING phrase.

For example, if DATA-1 has the value 100, then:

```
* Stores the value DATA-1 / 5, or 100 / 5, or 20,
* into DATA-2
  DIVIDE 5 INTO DATA-1 GIVING DATA-2.
```

Format 4 of the DIVIDE command functions in the same way as Format 3, except the REMAINDER phrase is included in this version.

The following list shows you a quick way to remember how the different formats of the DIVIDE command function:

+ **Format 1**: Divide A into B.

+ **Format 2**: Divide A into B giving C.

+ **Format 3**: Divide A by B giving C.

+ **Format 4**: Divide A into B giving C, remainder D.

+ **Format 5**: Divide A by B giving C, remainder D.

ENABLE

The ENABLE command starts transfers of information between input queues and destinations. The ENABLE command has the following format:

```
ENABLE
    {INPUT [TERMINAL] or I-O TERMINAL or OUTPUT} cd-name-1
    [WITH KEY {identifier-1 or literal-1}].
```

When using the ENABLE command, remember the following items:

+ If you use the INPUT phrase, cd-name-1 must refer to an input communication device. If the TERMINAL phrase is not also used, all sub-queues associated with the device are also started.

+ If you use the I-O TERMINAL phrase, cd-name-1 must refer to an input-output communication device.

+ If you use the OUTPUT phrase, cd-name-1 must refer to an output communication device.

+ To avoid turning on devices a program doesn't have access to, use the WITH KEY phrase. If the key contained in the literal or data item matches the system password for the device, then

the queue is enabled. Consult your system documentation for further information. (While this phrase is still part of ANSI-85 COBOL, it is scheduled to be removed from future versions. You should avoid using the WITH KEY phrase if possible.)

If you'd like to see an example of the ENABLE command which enables the output device, MY-DEVICE, look no further:

```
* Fire up MY-DEVICE
  ENABLE OUTPUT MY-DEVICE.
```

ENTER

The ENTER command embeds a routine or procedure written in another programming language into your COBOL program. The ENTER command has the following format:

ENTER *language-name-1* [*routine-name-1*].

While the ENTER command is still part of the ANSI-85 COBOL standard, it is scheduled to be removed in subsequent versions. You should try to avoid using this command if at all possible. Refer to your system and compiler specific information for further information about the other programming languages that are supported through the use of the enter command.

EXIT

The EXIT command provides an ending point for a group of procedures or a program. The EXIT command has the following two formats:

FORMAT 1:

EXIT.

FORMAT 2:

EXIT PROGRAM.

If you use Format 1 of the EXIT command, it specifies the end to a common set of procedures.

If you use Format 2 of the EXIT command, it specifies the end of a program that was called using the CALL command, returning control to the program that issued the CALL command.

In previous version of COBOL, the EXIT PROGRAM statement had to be the only command in a procedure. In ANSI-85 COBOL, the EXIT PROGRAM statement can now appear anywhere.

Can you handle an example of the EXIT command? Here goes:

```
PROCEDURE-1.
* Do some stuff here
  IF THIS-VALUE > THAT-VALUE GO TO PROCEDURE-4
  PROCEDURE-2.
* Do some other stuff here
  PROCEDURE-3.
* Do some more other stuff here
  PROCEDURE-4.
* Time to get out of here...
  EXIT.
```

GENERATE

The GENERATE command produces a report defined using the report writer definitions. The GENERATE command has the following format:

GENERATE {*data-name-1 or report-name-1*}.

When using the GENERATE command, keep the following points in mind:

+ The INITIATE command must be called before the report is generated.

+ Data-name-1 must name a detail report group.

+ Report-name-1 must refer to a report description entry that contains a CONTROL clause; report description entry doesn't contain more than one detail report group; report description entry contains at least one body group entry. (*See also* Part II for more information on defining a report.)

An example of the GENERATE command that fires up the report REPORT-1 follows:

```
* Let's call REPORT-1
  INITIATE REPORT-1.
  GENERATE REPORT-1.
```

GO TO

The GO TO command transfers control to a designated procedure. The GO TO command has the following format:

FORMAT 1:

```
GO TO [procedure-name-1].
```

FORMAT 2:

```
GO TO {procedure-name-1}...DEPENDING ON identifier-1.
```

If you use Format 1 of the GO TO command, control is simply transferred to procedure-name-1.

If you use Format 2 of the GO TO command, the following takes place:

+ Control is passed to one of the procedures specified, based on the value of identifier-1. Identifier-1 must be an integer.

+ If identifier-1 has the value of 1, then control is passed to the first procedure name specified in the GO TO command; if it's 2, then the second procedure, and so on. If the value of identifier-1 is greater than the number of procedure names specified, or zero, then the GO TO command is simply ignored.

In the following code, you get an up-close-and-personal example of the GO TO command:

```
* Let's play roulette!
  GO TO ROULETTE-TABLE-1 ROULETTE-TABLE-2
        ROULETTE-TABLE-3
  DEPENDING ON TABLE-VALUE.
```

Programmers have a raging debate about the use of the GO TO statement. The prevailing wisdom is that the GO TO statement should be avoided. In any well-structured program, you should not need the GO TO statement.

IF

The IF command controls the flow of execution based on a condition. The IF statement can execute one set of statements if the condition is logically true, and another set of statements if the condition is logically false. The IF command has the following format:

```
IF condition-1
THEN {{statement-1}... or
      NEXT SENTENCE}
{ELSE {statement-2...[END-IF] or
      ELSE NEXT SENTENCE or
      END-IF}.
```

When using the IF command, condition-1 can be any of the condition types support by COBOL (relation, class, condition name, sign, or switch condition). If condition-1 is true, then the commands following the THEN phrase are executed; otherwise, if the ELSE phrase is included, the commands following the ELSE phrase are executed. When the NEXT SENTENCE phrase appears in either the THEN or ELSE section of the IF command, control is passed to the command that follows the IF command. The NEXT SENTENCE and ELSE phrases are optional.

The following code shows you an example of the IF command that uses the ELSE phrase:

```
* If ITEM-1 is > 5 add 10 to COUNTER,
* otherwise subtract 12 from COUNTER
  IF ITEM-1 > 5 THEN
    ADD 10 TO COUNTER
  ELSE
    SUBTRACT 12 FROM COUNTER
  END-IF.
```

INITIALIZE

The INITIALIZE command stores initial values in a data item. (The INITIALIZE command is new to the ANSI-85 COBOL standard.) The INITIALIZE command has the following format:

```
INITIALIZE {identifier-1}...
[REPLACING
 {{ALPHABETIC or
   ALPHANUMERIC or
   NUMERIC or
   ALPHANUMERIC-EDITED or
   NUMERIC-EDITED}
DATA BY {identifier-2 or literal-1}}...].
```

When using the INITIALIZE command, if the data item, identifier-1, is a numeric type, it is initialized to zero; if it is an alphanumeric type, it is set to spaces. The REPLACING...BY phrase specifies a different initialization value. If a type is specified after the replacing phrase, the value will only be initialized to the value specified by the REPLACING...BY phrase if it is of the same type. More than one REPLACING...BY phrase can be specified for an INITIALIZE command.

I know it's not your birthday, but I decided to give you some examples of INITIALIZE commands in action anyway:

```
* Set THIS-ITEM to zeros or spaces, whatever is
* appropriate for its type
  INITIALIZE THIS-ITEM.
* Set THAT-ITEM to XXXXXX if it is an alphanumeric type
  INITIALIZE THAT-ITEM
    REPLACING ALPHANUMERIC BY "XXXXXX".
```

INITIATE

The INITIATE command begins the processing of a report. The INITIATE command has the following format:

```
INITIATE {report-name-1}...
```

When using the INITIATE command, keep the following points in mind:

✦ The sum counter is reset to 0, the line counter is reset to zero, and the page counter is reset to 0.

✦ Multiple report names can be specified with the INITIATE command.

✦ A report name can't be initiated again until the TERMINATE command is called.

Behold, the following code, which shows you an example of the INITIATE command:

```
* Start Running REPORT-1 and REPORT-2
  INITIATE REPORT-1 REPORT-2.
```

INSPECT

The INSPECT command counts or replaces the occurrences of a character or group of characters in a data item. The INSPECT command has the following four formats:

FORMAT 1:

```
INSPECT identifier-1 TALLYING
  {identifier-2 FOR
    {CHARACTERS [{BEFORE or AFTER} INITIAL
      {identifier-4 or literal-2}]... or
    {ALL or LEADING} {{identifier-3 or
                      literal-1} [{BEFORE or AFTER}
                      INITIAL {identifier-4 or
                      literal-2}]...}...}...}...
```

FORMAT 2:

```
INSPECT identifier-1 REPLACING
  {CHARACTERS BY {identifier-5 or literal-3}
    [{BEFORE or AFTER} INITIAL
      {identifier-4 or literal-2}]... or
  {ALL or LEADING or FIRST} {{identifier-3 or literal-1}
    BY {identifier-5 or literal-3}
    [{BEFORE or AFTER} INITIAL
      {identifier-4 or literal-2}]...}...}...
```

FORMAT 3:

```
INSPECT identifier-1 TALLYING
  {identifier-2 FOR
    {CHARACTERS [{BEFORE or AFTER} INITIAL
      {identifier-4 or literal-2}]... or
    {ALL or LEADING}
      {{identifier-3 or literal-1}
      [{BEFORE or AFTER} INITIAL
        {identifier-4 or literal-2}]...}...}...}...
  REPLACING
    {CHARACTERS BY {identifier-5 or literal-3}
    [{BEFORE or AFTER} INITIAL
      {identifier-4 or literal-2}]... or
    {ALL or LEADING or FIRST}
      {{identifier-3 or literal-1} BY
      {identifier-5 or literal-3}
      [{BEFORE or AFTER} INITIAL
        {identifier-4 or literal-2}]...}...}...
```

FORMAT 4:

```
INSPECT identifier-1 CONVERTING
  {identifier-6 or literal-4} TO
  {identifier-7 or literal-5}
  [{BEFORE or AFTER} INITIAL
  {identifier-4 or literal-2}]...
```

When using Format 1 of the INSPECT command, the TALLYING phrase counts the number of characters in the data item, identifier-1, that are in the specified range. The count of characters is stored in the data item identifier-2.

If you use the BEFORE phrase, all characters that are before the value specified in identifier-4 or literal-1 are counted.

If you use the AFTER phrase, all characters that are before the value specified in identifier-4 or literal-1 are counted.

If you use the ALL phrase, then the number of occurrences of the character or string specified in the data item identifer-3 or literal-1 are counted.

If the LEADING phrase is specified, then the number of times the character or string specified in the data item identifer-3 or literal-1 are counted when they appear at the beginning of the data item identifier-1.

If the CHARACTERS phrase appears alone, then the number of characters in the data item, identifer-1, are simply counted.

Take a close look at an example of the INSPECT command using the TALLYING phrase:

```
* Count strings in ITEM-1
  INSPECT ITEM-1 TALLYING COUNT-1 FOR ALL "AB"
                          COUNT-2 FOR ALL "D"
                          COUNT-3 FOR LEADING "BE"
                          COUNT-4 FOR CHARACTERS.
```

The following table shows the value of the COUNT data items for varying values of the ITEM-1 data item:

ITEM-1	COUNT-1	COUNT-2	COUNT-3	COUNT-4
BABABAC	2	0	0	7
BEFRSTUWXYZ	0	0	1	11

If you use Format 2 of the INSPECT command, instead of counting the number of occurrences of a character or string, they are replaced instead. The BEFORE, AFTER, CHARACTERS, and LEADING phrases operate in the same way as they do in Format 1.

The following example shows the INSPECT command using the REPLACING phrase:

```
* Replace strings in ITEM-1
  INSPECT ITEM-1 REPLACING ALL "A" BY "B".
```

The following table shows the value of the ITEM-1 data item before and after the replacements:

ITEM-1 Before	ITEM-1 After
BABABAC	AAAAAAC
BEFRSTUWXYZ	AEFRSTUWXYZ

Format 3 of the INSPECT command combines the TALLYING phrase of Format 1, with the REPLACING phrase of Format 2.

Format 4 of the INSPECT command is new to the ANSI-85 COBOL standard. It is the same as Format 2 of the INSPECT command, except that the ALL phrase is implied.

MERGE

The MERGE command combines the contents of two or more files using a specific set of keys. The MERGE command has the following format:

```
MERGE file-name-1
  {ON {ASCENDING or DESCENDING} KEY {data-name-1}...}...
  [COLLATING SEQUENCE IS alphabet-name-1]
```

USING *file-name-2* {*file-name-3*}...
{OUTPUT PROCEDURE IS *procedure-name-1*
    [{THROUGH *or* THRU} *procedure-name-2*] *or*
GIVING {*file-name-4*}...}.

When using the MERGE command, you should remember the following items:

+ File-name-1, file-name-2, file-name-3, and file-name-4 must be defined in a sort-merge file description. File-name-1 specifies the resulting data file. The file names specified after the USING phrase are the input data files.

+ Data-name-1 must be a data item defined in the record description entry of file-name-1.

+ The records of file-name-2 and file-name-3 must be arranged in the order as specified in the ASCENDING KEY or DESCENDING KEY phrase.

+ If the OUTPUT PROCEDURE phrase is written, control passes to the output procedure upon completion of the merge operation. The output procedure specified must be declared in the PROCEDURE DIVISION's declarative section.

+ When you omit the COLLATING SEQUENCE phrase, use the system collating sequence. Otherwise the collating sequence specified is used.

+ If the GIVING phrase is written, the merged records become available for use as those in file-name-1 and are written to the file named by file-name-4.

An example of the MERGE command follows:

```
* Merge the file FILE-1 and FILE-2 together using the
* ascending key KEY-1 producing the file FILE-3
  MERGE FILE-3 ON ASCENDING KEY-1 USING FILE-1 FILE-2.
```

FILE-1 and FILE-2 are defined in the DATA DIVISION using the SD directive. *See also* Part IV for more information on the DATA DIVISION.

MOVE

The MOVE command moves the contents of a data item or literal into another data item. The MOVE command has the following format:

FORMAT 1:

MOVE {*identifier-1 or literal-3*} **TO** {*identifier-2*}...

FORMAT 2:

```
MOVE {CORRESPONDING or CORR} identifier-1 TO
    identifier-2.
```

While the MOVE command is pretty much straightforward — it moves a value from one location to another — you need to understand a few rules that come into play depending on the type of the values:

✦ When moving alphanumeric type values, characters are transferred from left to right. If the receiving data item is longer than the source data item, the receiving data item is padded with spaces. If the receiving data item is shorter than the source data item, the receiving data is filled to its length, and the rest of the characters are discarded. Finally, a numeric or numeric-edited item can't be moved to an alphabetic item.

✦ When moving numeric values, if the values contain a decimal point, the values are moved preserving the decimal point. If the source data item is signed, then it is moved to the destination. If the source data item is alphanumeric, then it is treated as an unsigned numeric.

✦ When moving elementary data items, any data conversion that is required is automatically performed.

✦ When moving group data items, items are treated as alphanumeric, and no conversion is performed.

What could be more perfect than the example of the MOVE command that follows:

```
* Move 1234 to NUM-1
  MOVE 1234 TO NUM-1.
* Move ITEM-1 to ITEM-2
  MOVE ITEM-1 TO ITEM-2.
```

MULTIPLY

The MULTIPLY command multiplies two data items together and stores the result in one or more data items. The MULTIPLY command has the following two formats:

FORMAT 1:

```
MULTIPLY {identifier-1 or literal-1} BY
    {identifier-2 [ROUNDED]}...
    [ON SIZE ERROR imperative-statement-1]
[NOT ON SIZE ERROR imperative-statement-2]
[END-MULTIPLY].
```

FORMAT 2:

```
MULTIPLY {identifier-1 or literal-1} BY
    {identifier-2 or literal-2}
GIVING {identifier-3} [ROUNDED]}...
    [ON SIZE ERROR imperative-statement-1]
[NOT ON SIZE ERROR imperative-statement-2]
[END-MULTIPLY].
```

When using Format 1 of the MULTIPLY command, the numeric value in identifier-1 or literal-1 is multiplied to the value stored in identifier-2, and the result is stored in identifier-2.

For example, if DATA-1 has the value 100, then:

```
* Stores DATA-1 * 5, or 100 * 5, or 500 in DATA-1
  MULTIPLY 5 BY DATA-1.
```

Format 2 of the MULTIPLY command functions in the same way as Format 1, except the result is stored in the data item specified after the GIVING phrase.

For example, if DATA-1 has the value 100, then:

```
* Stores the value DATA-1 * 5, or 100 * 5, or 500,
* into DATA-2
  MULTIPLY 5 BY DATA-1 GIVING DATA-2.
```

OPEN

The OPEN command makes a file available for processing. The first operation on any file must be an OPEN command. The OPEN command has the following three formats:

FORMAT 1:

```
OPEN
 {INPUT {file-name-1 [REVERSED or WITH NO REWIND]}... or
  OUTPUT {file-name-2 [WITH NO REWIND]}... or
  I-O {file-name-3}... or
  EXTEND {file-name-4}...}...
```

FORMAT 2:

```
OPEN
  {INPUT {file-name-1}... or
   OUTPUT {file-name-2}... or
   I-O {file-name-3}... or
   EXTEND {file-name-4}...}...
```

FORMAT 3:

```
OPEN
  {OUTPUT {file-name-1 [WITH NO REWIND]}... or
   EXTEND {file-name-2}...
```

When using the OPEN command, keep open minded about the following items:

✦ If you use the INPUT phrase, the file specified is opened for input only; if the OUTPUT phrase is specified, the file is opened for output only. If the INPUT-OUTPUT phrase is specified, the file is opened for both input and output. If the EXTEND phrase is specified, the file is open for output, and the file cursor is positioned at the end of the file, ready for appending. Also, the EXTEND phrase is only allowed for sequential access files if the new data is written in ascending sequence.

✦ The file name specified by the OPEN command must be defined in the DATA DIVISION.

✦ If the REVERSED phrase is specified, when the file is opened, it is positioned at the end. When READ commands are executed, records are read in reverse order (from the end of the file to the beginning of the file).

✦ If the NO REWIND phrase is specified, the current file is not at the beginning of the file when the file is opened. The file must be positioned before it can be READ. (The NO REWIND phrase relates back to the days when files were stored and read from tape, the phrase prevented the tape from being reminded before the file was read. If you're using a file stored on a tape, remember that only one file on a tape can be opened at a time, and only the last file on a tape can be opened for output.)

The following code shows you an example of the OPEN command:

```
* Open FILE-1 for input in reverse order and FILE-2
* for output
  OPEN INPUT FILE-1 REVERSED
  OPEN OUTPUT FILE-2.
```

PERFORM

The PERFORM command executes one or more paragraphs or statements within the command. The PERFORM command has the following four formats:

```
FORMAT 1:

PERFORM [procedure-name-1
  [{THROUGH or THRU} procedure-name-2]]
[imperative-statement-1 END-PERFORM].
```

FORMAT 2:

```
PERFORM [procedure-name-1
   [{THROUGH or THRU} procedure-name-2]]
   {identifier-1 or integer-1} TIMES
[imperative-statement-1 END-PERFORM].
```

FORMAT 3:

```
PERFORM [procedure-name-1
   [{THROUGH or THRU} procedure-name-2]]
   [WITH TEST {BEFORE or AFTER}] UNTIL condition-1
[imperative-statement-1 END-PERFORM].
```

FORMAT 4:

```
PERFORM [procedure-name-1
   [{THROUGH or THRU} procedure-name-2]]
[WITH TEST {BEFORE or AFTER}]
   VARYING {identifier-4 or literal-1}
   FROM {identifier-3 or index-name-2 or literal-1}
   BY {identifier-4 or literal-2} UNTIL
      condition-1
   [AFTER {identifier-5 or index-name-3} FROM
      {identifier-6 or index-name-4 or literal-3}
   BY {identifier-7 or literal-4} UNTIL
      condition-2]...
[imperative-statement-1 END-PERFORM].
```

When using the PERFORM command, keep the following points in mind:

✦ If the THROUGH or THRU phrase is specified, the procedure or range of procedures specified is executed, and when complete, control returns to the command following the PERFORM command.

✦ If the TIMES phrase is specified, the specified procedure or range of procedures is executed that many times in a row.

✦ If the UNTIL phrase is specified, the specified procedure or range of procedures is executed until the specified condition is true. Using the TEST BEFORE and AFTER phrases, you can control when the test is performed.

✦ If the VARYING phrase is specified, the procedure or range of procedures is executed as the value of the data item is incremented by the value specified after the BY phrase until the specified condition is true.

The PERFORM command in action looks a little something like the following code:

```
*  Just run PROCEDURE-1
   PERFORM PROCEDURE-1.
*  Run PROCEDURE-2 5 times
   PERFORM PROCEDURE-2
      5 TIMES
   END-PERFORM.
*  Run PROCEDURE-3 until X is greater than 10
   PERFORM PROCEDURE-3
      UNTIL X > 10
   END-PERFORM.
*  Run PROCEDURE-4 incrementing X by 2 until X is greater
*  than 10
   PERFORM PROCEDURE-4
      VARYING X BY 2
      UNTIL X > 10
   END-PERFORM.
```

Phrases

A number of COBOL commands use *verb phrases* (clauses that are part of a command). For example, the ADD, SUBTRACT, MULTIPLY, DIVIDE, and MOVE commands use the ROUNDED, ON SIZE ERROR, and CORRESPONDING phrases.

The number of the decimal places created as the result of arithmetic operation may be more than can be stored in the resulting data item. The following processing is performed depending on whether the ROUNDED phrase is present:

+ Without the ROUNDED phrase, the fraction part obtained by the arithmetic operation is truncated by the length of the resulting data item.

+ With the ROUNDED phrase, the least significant digit of the resultant identifier is increased by 1 when the most significant digit of the excess is greater than or equal to 5.

ON SIZE ERROR

An arithmetic statement may cause a size error condition, which can be intercepted when the ON SIZE ERROR phrase is included in the arithmetic statement. A size error condition can occur when:

+ The result of evaluating an exponent is not a real number.

+ The divisor is zero.

+ The absolute value obtained by an operation is greater than the maximum value that can be stored in the resulting data item.

After completion of the arithmetic operation, that is, after all the values of resultant identifiers have been determined, control is transferred according to the following rules:

✦ Control is transferred to an imperative statement in which the ON SIZE ERROR phrase is written. After the statement is executed, control is transferred to the end of the arithmetic statement. However, in the imperative statement, a procedure branching statement or a conditional statement that causes explicit control transfer may be executed. If so, control is transferred according to the rules of the statement.

✦ Without the ON SIZE ERROR phrase, control is transferred to the end of the arithmetic statement.

CORRESPONDING

You can include the MOVE, ADD, or SUBTRACT statements when using the CORRESPONDING phrase. The CORRESPONDING phrase associates data items with the same name that belong to the same data item group.

The CORRESPONDING phrase simplifies programming when the same operation is to be performed on one or several pairs of elementary, non-unique data names.

For example, suppose the following two records were defined:

```
01 PAY-RECORD.
   02 GROSS    PIC 99999V99.
   02 NET      PIC 99999V99.
   02 WITHHOLD PIC 9999V99.
01 EDITED-PAY-RECORD.
   02 GROSS    PIC ZZZZ9.99.
   02 NET      PIC ZZZ9.99.
   02 WITHHOLD PIC ZZZ9.99.
```

If you want to move the contents of PAY-RECORD to EDITED-PAY-RECORD, you can't just write MOVE PAY-RECORD TO EDITED-PAY-RECORD because this is invalid. You can only MOVE or perform arithmetic operations on elementary data items. With a little magic from the CORRESPONDING phrase, you can MOVE or perform arithmetic operations on group data items. For example, you can use the command MOVE CORRESPONDING PAY-RECORD TO EDITED-PAY-RECORD to move the contents of PAY-RECORD group data items to the EDITED-PAY-RECORD group data items.

When using the CORRESPONDING phrase, you must have pairs of data items in the two groups that have the same names. Any items that are subordinate to the group data items that are defined using the RENAMES, REDEFINES, or OCCURS phrases are ignored in the operation that uses the CORRESPONDING phrase.

PURGE

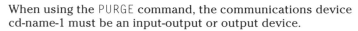

The PURGE command removes a partial message from a communications queue. The PURGE command has the following format:

```
PURGE cd-name-1.
```

When using the PURGE command, the communications device cd-name-1 must be an input-output or output device.

The following code presents an example of the PURGE command:

```
* Dump the output queue
  PURGE OUTPUT-QUEUE.
```

READ

The READ command reads a record from a file and stores the result in a data item. When reading sequential files, the next record in the file is read. When reading an indexed or relative file, you specify a record to be read. The READ command has the following three formats:

FORMAT 1:

```
READ file-name-1 [NEXT] RECORD [INTO identifier-1]
[AT END imperative-statement-1]
[NOT AT END imperative-statement-2]
[END-READ].
```

FORMAT 2:

```
READ file-name-1 RECORD [INTO identifier-1]
[INVALID KEY imperative-statement-1]
[NOT INVALID KEY imperative-statement-2]
[END-READ].
```

FORMAT 3:

```
READ file-name-1 RECORD [INTO identifier-1]
[KEY IS data-name-1]
[INVALID KEY imperative-statement-1]
[NOT INVALID KEY imperative-statement-2]
[END-READ].
```

When using the READ command, keep the following points in mind:

◆ File-name-1 must be defined in the DATA DIVISION. (**See also** Part IV for more information on the DATA DIVISION.)

◆ If the INTO phrase is specified, the record read from the file is transferred into the data item identifier-1.

✦ If the END phrase is specified, the command specified after the END phrase is executed after the end of the file is reached. If the NOT END phrase is specified, then the command specified after the NOT END phrase is executed until the end of the file is reached.

✦ If the KEY phrase is specified, then the record having the specified key is read. The KEY phrase can only be used with indexed and relative files.

✦ If the INVALID phrase is specified and an invalid key is specified using the KEY phrase, then the command following the INVALID phrase is executed. If the NOT INVALID phrase is specified and a valid key is specified using the KEY phrase, then the command following the NOT INVALID phrase is executed.

An example of the READ command follows:

```
* Just read a record from FILE-1 into the file's
* associated data area
  READ FILE-1.
* Read a record from FILE-2 into the DATA-AREA data item
  READ FILE-2 INTO DATA-AREA.
* Read the record matching KEY-1 from FILE-3
  READ FILE-3 KEY KEY-1.
```

RECEIVE

The RECEIVE command makes a message available to a program and has the following format:

RECEIVE *cd-name-1* {MESSAGE *or* SEGMENT} INTO *identifier-1*
[NO DATA *imperative-statement-1*]
[WITH DATA *imperative-statement-2*]
[END-RECEIVE].

When using the RECEIVE command, the communications device specified by cd-name-1 must be an input or input-output device. The contents of the message received are stored in the data item, identifier-1. If you use the NO DATA phrase, and data is not received, then the statement following the NO DATA phrase is executed. If you use the DATA phrase, and data is received, then the statement following the DATA phrase is executed.

The following code shows you an example of the RECEIVE command:

```
* Get some data from the INPUT-QUEUE, calling the
* GOT-DATA procedure when data is received
  RECEIVE INPUT-QUEUE MESSAGE INTO THIS-MESSAGE
    DATA PERFORM GOT-DATA
  END-RECEIVE.
```

RELEASE

The RELEASE command delivers a record to the first step of a sorting operation. The RELEASE command has the following format:

RELEASE *record-name-1* [FROM *identifier-1*].

The RELEASE command can only be used in the input procedure associated with a SORT command. The RELEASE command allows a record to be sorted by the SORT command. After the RELEASE command is executed, the data contained in the record, record-name-1, is no longer valid. If the FROM phrase is specified, the contents of the data item identifier-1 are moved to the record, record-name-1, before the record is released.

Take a look at the following example of the RELEASE command:

```
* Once the input sort processing is complete...
  RELEASE SORT-RECORD.
```

RETURN

The RETURN command receives the sorted or merged record from the last step of a sort or merge operation. The RETURN command has the following format:

```
RETURN file-name-1 RECORD [INTO identifier-1]
AT END imperative-statement-1
[NOT AT END imperative-statement-2]
[END-RETURN].
```

The RETURN command can only be used in the input procedure associated with a SORT command. When the RETURN command is executed, the next record is made available to the SORT command.

If the INTO phrase is specified, the contents of the current record are moved to the data item, identifier-1, before the record is returned. If the END phrase is specified, when end of the file is reached, the statement following the phrase is executed. If the NOT END phrase is specified, the statement following the phrase is executed until the end of the file is reached.

REWRITE

The REWRITE command replaces the contents of the current record in a file. The REWRITE command has the following two formats:

FORMAT 1:

REWRITE *record-name-1* [**FROM** *identifier-1*] [**END-REWRITE**].

FORMAT 2:

REWRITE *record-name-1* [**FROM** *identifier-1*]
[**INVALID** KEY *imperative-statement-1*]
[**NOT INVALID** KEY *imperative-statement-2*]
[**END-REWRITE**].

When using either format of the REWRITE command, try to remember the following items:

✦ The record-name-1 must be the name of the record defined in the file section of the data division. The file must be open for output or input-output mode.

✦ When a data item is specified in identifier-1, the same area must not be specified for record-name-1.

When using Format 2 of the REWRITE command, if an invalid key condition occurs during execution of the REWRITE command, the command will fail. The record area of the file related to record-name-1 remains unchanged, and the statement following the INVALID KEY phrase is executed.

In the following example, I show you one way to use the REWRITE command:

```
* Update the current record in UPDATE-FILE , handle an
* invalid key situation
  REWRITE UPDATE-FILE
     INVALID KEY PERFORM BAD-KEY-ROUTINE
  END-REWRITE.
```

SEARCH

The SEARCH command scans a table for an element that meets conditions that you specify. The SEARCH command has the following two formats:

FORMAT 1:

```
SEARCH identifier-1
  [VARYING {identifier-2 or index-name-1}]
[AT END imperative-statement-1]
  {WHEN condition-1
    {imperative-statement-2 or NEXT SENTENCE}}...
[END-SEARCH].
```

FORMAT 2:

```
SEARCH ALL identifier-1
  [AT END imperative-statement-1]
  WHEN {data-name-1 {IS EQUAL TO or IS =}
       {identifier-3 or literal-1 or
        arithmetic-expression-1} or condition name-1}
  [AND {data-name-2 {IS EQUAL TO or IS =}
       {identifier-4 or literal-2 or
        arithmetic-expression-2} or condition-name-2}]...
  {imperative-statement-2 or NEXT SENTENCE}
[END-SEARCH].
```

When using the SEARCH command, keep the following points in mind:

+ Identifier-1 must be a table.

+ If the VARYING phrase is specified, the specified index item is varied as the search proceeds through the table.

+ If the END phrase is specified, then the command specified after the phrase is executed when the end of the table is reached.

+ If the WHEN phrase is specified, if the condition specified is true, the command specified after the WHEN phrase is executed for each data element searched. If the NEXT SEN-TENCE phrase is specified, execution just continues.

+ The AND phrase can be used to specify multiple WHEN phrases. If the ALL phrase is specified, the SEARCH terminates only when ALL of the WHEN conditions are true.

+ Format 1 uses a linear search; each data item is searched in order until the data item is found.

+ Format 2 uses a binary search, which can be much faster, but the data items in the table must be in sorted order.

SEND

The SEND command sends a message to one or more output communication devices. The SEND command has the following two formats:

FORMAT 1:

```
SEND cd-name-1 FROM identifier-1.
```

FORMAT 2:

```
SEND cd-name-1 [FROM identifier-1]
  {WITH identifier-2 or
   WITH ESI or
   WITH EMI or
   WITH EGI}
   [{BEFORE or AFTER} ADVANCING
    {{identifier-3 or integer-1} [LINE or LINES] or
     {mnemonic-name-1 or PAGE}}]
[REPLACING LINE].
```

Format 1 of the SEND command sends the data contained in the data-item, identifier-1, to the communications device specified by cd-name-1. The communications device specified by cd-name-1 must be an output or input-output communications device.

Format 2 of the SEND command also sends a message. Optional indicators and line feeds can also be sent. If you specify the WITH ESI phrase, an end of segment indicator is sent. If you specify the WITH EMI phrase, an end of message indicator is sent. If the WITH EGI phrase is specified, an end of group indicator is sent. The BEFORE or AFTER ADVANCING phrase can be included to send one or more line feeds. If the REPLACING phrase is specified, the information currently in the queue is replaced.

An example of a simple SEND command follows:

```
* Send the message THIS-MESSAGE to the output device
* DEVICE-1
  SEND DEVICE-1 FROM THIS-MESSAGE.
```

SET

The SET command stores or changes the value of a table index, mnemonic name, or condition name. The SET command has the following four formats:

FORMAT 1:

```
SET {index-name-1 or identifier-1}...
  TO {index-name-2 or identifier-2 or integer-1}.
```

FORMAT 2:

```
SET {index-name-3}...
  {UP BY or DOWN BY} {identifier-3 or integer-2}.
```

FORMAT 3:

```
SET {{mnemonic-name-1}...TO {ON or OFF}}...
```

FORMAT 4:

```
SET {condition-name-1}...TO TRUE.
```

When using the SET command in Format 1 or Format 2, the index value for a table is set:

+ Identifier-1 and identifier-2 must be index data items or integer items. Identifier-1 must be a non-zero, positive integer.

+ Identifier-3 must be an integer item.

+ Format 1 stores the value in index-name-2, identifier-2, or the literal integer-1 to the value specified by index-name-1 or identifier-1.

+ Format 2 increments or decrements the index value index-name-3 by the value specified after the UP BY or DOWN BY phrase.

When using the SET command in Format 3, the external switch specified by mnemonic-name-1 is set ON or OFF. (**See also** Part III for more information on creating mnemonic names.)

When using the SET command in Format 4, the condition name specified by condition-name-1 is set to TRUE or FALSE.

Typically, you use Format 1 of the SET command for basic table handling, Format 2 for adjusting indexes, Format 3 for setting external switches, and Format 4 for setting condition names.

The following example shows you a SET command which sets THIS-INDEX to 5 and increments THAT-INDEX by 2:

```
* Set THIS-INDEX to 5
  SET THIS-INDEX TO 5.
* Increment THAT-INDEX by 2
  SET THAT-INDEX UP BY 2.
```

SORT

The SORT command sorts a file in a specific order based on a set of specified keys. The SORT command has the following format:

```
SORT file-name-1
  {ON {ASCENDING or DESCENDING} KEY {data-name-1}...}...
[WITH DUPLICATES IN ORDER]
[COLLATING SEQUENCE IS alphabet-name-1]
  {INPUT PROCEDURE IS procedure-name-1
    [{THROUGH or THRU} procedure-name-2} or
  USING {file-name-2}...
  {OUTPUT PROCEDURE IS procedure-name-3
    [{THROUGH or THRU} procedure-name-4} or
 GIVING {file-name-3}...
```

When using the SORT command, remember the following points:

✦ File-name-1 specifies the name of the file to sort and must be defined in the DATA DIVISION as a sort merge file. File-name-2 and file-name-3 must not be open when the sort command is executed, and they must be defined using a record size large enough to hold the contents of a file-name-1 record. (In versions prior to the ANSI-85 COBOL standard, file-name-2 and file-name-3 had to be defined as sequential files; this is no longer required.) File-name-2 and file-name-3 can't be defined as sort-merge files.

✦ The ASCENDING clause specifies a record key. The records in the file will be sorted in ascending order (lowest to highest) based on the value of the key. If you use the DESCENDING clause, the records in the file will be sorted in descending order (from highest to lowest) based on the value of the key. The key data item must be defined as a data item in file-name-1; it can't be a group data item. The key data item must be defined in the fixed length area of file-name-1 if file-name-1 is a variable length file.

✦ The WITH DUPLICATES clause specifies how records with duplicate key values are treated. If the clause is specified, records containing duplicate key values are written in the same order they were originally in file-name-1. If the WITH DUPLICATES phrase is not specified, the order of records with duplicate keys is not defined.

✦ The SEQUENCE clause specifies an alternate alphabet to use when sorting the file (***see also*** Part III for more information on defining alphabets in the ENVIRONMENT DIVISION). If the SEQUENCE clause is not specified, the default alphabet is used when sorting.

✦ If you specify the INPUT PROCEDURE clause, the procedure or range of procedures specified are called immediately before the sorting process begins. These procedures can be used for file pre-processing.

✦ If you specify the OUTPUT PROCEDURE clause, the procedure or range of procedures specified are called immediately after the sorting process begins. These procedures can be used for file post-processing.

✦ The USING clause is used when records are made available to the sort from file-name-2 without any processing.

✦ The GIVING clause is used to specify the file where the sorted records will be written.

The following example demonstrates how to use the SORT command to order a file in ascending order based on the key data item:

```
* Sort the Customer file in ascending order based on
* the Customer Name
  SORT CUST-FILE
     ASCENDING KEY CUST-NAME
     GIVING SORTED-CUST-FILE.
```

START

The START command sets the current record position of a relative or indexed before a record is read. The START command has the following format:

```
START file-name-1
   [KEY (IS EQUAL TO or
         IS = or
         IS GREATER THAN or
         IS > or
         IS NOT LESS THAN or
         IS NOT < or
         IS GREATER THAN OR EQUAL TO or
         IS >=) data-name-1]
[INVALID KEY imperative-statement-1]
[NOT INVALID KEY imperative-statement-2]
[END-START].
```

When using the START command, keep the following points in mind:

+ The file-name-1 must be a file opened in sequential or dynamic access mode.

+ The data item, data-name-1, must be the data item (relative key item) written in the RELATIVE KEY phrase of the ACCESS MODE clause in the file control entry related to file-name-1. The data item, data-name-1, can be qualified. (*See also* Part II for more information on qualification and defining relative keys.)

+ The file assigned to file-name-1 must be opened in input mode or I-O mode before the START command is executed.

+ If the KEY phrase isn't used, the relation IS EQUAL TO is assumed.

+ Even after the START command has been executed, the contents in the record area of file-name-1 don't change.

+ If the key specified is invalid, then the statement after the INVALID KEY phrase is executed. This statement can provide any special processing when an invalid key is encountered.

◆ If the key specified is valid, then the statement after the NOT INVALID KEY phrase is executed. This statement can provide any special processing when an valid key is encountered.

An example of the START command which moves to a specific key follows:

```
* Move to the record identified by KEY-1
  MOVE "9912567" TO KEY-1
  START THIS-FILE
    KEY IS EQUAL TO KEY-1
  END-START.
```

STOP

The STOP command terminates the executing of a program. The STOP command has the following format:

```
STOP {RUN or literal-1}.
```

When using the STOP command, remember the following items:

◆ When the STOP RUN command has been executed, control is transferred to the operating system.

◆ If files remain open during execution of the STOP RUN command, they are all closed.

◆ If you have a STOP RUN statement in which a value for literal-1 is specified, execution of the run unit is interrupted and the value of literal-1 is reported to the operator. While this version of the STOP statement is still available in ANSI-85 COBOL, it is scheduled to be removed from upcoming versions of the COBOL language. You should avoid using this form of the command if possible.

Take a look at the following example of the STOP command:

```
* I've had it!!
  STOP RUN.
```

STRING

The STRING command combines two or more data items storing the result in another data item. (STRING is the opposite of the UNSTRING command.) The STRING command has the following format:

```
STRING {{identifier-1 or literal-1}...
  DELIMITED BY {identifier-2 or literal-2 or SIZE}}...
  INTO identifier-3
[WITH POINTER identifier-4]
[ON OVERFLOW imperative-statement-1]
[NOT ON OVERFLOW imperative-statement-2]
[END-STRING].
```

When using the STRING command, remain aware of the following points:

✦ Literal-1 and literal-2 must be nonnumeric literals.

✦ Identifier-3 must not be an alphanumeric edited data item or a numeric edited data item. Identifier-3 also must not be a data item in which the JUSTIFIED clause has been specified.

✦ Identifier-4 must be an integer.

✦ The data items specified after the STRING command will be stored with the data item specified after the INTO phrase.

✦ If the DELIMITED phrase is specified, it is followed by a character that delineates each item as stored in the data item specified after the INTO phrase. Items are retrieved from identifier-1 and placed into the identifiers specified after the INTO phrase. If the DELIMITED phrase is not specified, each identifier specified after the INTO phrase is filled to its length before the next item is filled.

✦ The value specified after the POSITION command indicates the character position where the data items being strung together will be stored in the data item specified after the INTO phrase.

✦ If the OVERFLOW phrase is specified, the statement that follows will be executed if you have more characters in the data items being strung together than can fit in the destination data item. If all the characters fit in the destination data item, then the statement following the NOT OVERFLOW phrase is executed if it's included.

The following code presents an example of the STRING command:

```
* String'em up!
  STRING DATA-1 DATA-2 DATA-3
    INTO MY-DATA
  END-STRING.
```

If the data item, DATA-1, contained 1234, and the data item, DATA-2, contained ABCDE, and the data item, DATA-3, contained 999, then after executing the STRING command, the data item, MY-DATA, would contain 1234ABCDE999.

SUBTRACT

The SUBTRACT command subtracts the value of one of the sum of multiple data items from one or more data items. The SUBTRACT command has the following three formats:

FORMAT 1:

```
SUBTRACT {identifier-1 or literal-1}...
   FROM {identifier-2 [ROUNDED]}...
   [ON SIZE ERROR imperative-statement-1]
[NOT ON SIZE ERROR imperative-statement-2]
[END-SUBTRACT].
```

FORMAT 2:

```
SUBTRACT {identifier-1 or literal-1}...
   FROM {identifier-2 or literal-2}
   GIVING {identifier-3 [ROUNDED]}...
   [ON SIZE ERROR imperative-statement-1]
[NOT ON SIZE ERROR imperative-statement-2]
[END-SUBTRACT].
```

FORMAT 3:

```
SUBTRACT {CORRESPONDING or CORR} identifier-1
   FROM {identifier-2 [ROUNDED]}...
   [ON SIZE ERROR imperative-statement-1]
[NOT ON SIZE ERROR imperative-statement-2]
[END-SUBTRACT].
```

When using Format 1 of the SUBTRACT command, the numeric value in identifier-1 or literal-1 is subtracted from the value stored in identifier-2, and the result is stored in identifier-2. If more than one identifier or literal is specified before the FROM phrase, these values are summed and then subtracted from identifier-2.

Format 3 of the SUBTRACT command includes the CORRESPOND-ING phrase, but is otherwise the same as Format 1.

For example, if DATA-1 has the value 100, then:

```
* Stores DATA-1 - 5, or 100 - 5, or 95 in DATA-1
  SUBTRACT 5 FROM DATA-1.
* Stores DATA-1 - (5 + 5), or 95 - 10, or 85, in DATA-1
  SUBTRACT 5 5 FROM DATA-1.
```

Format 2 of the SUBTRACT command functions in the same way as Format 1, except the result is stored in the data item specified after the GIVING phrase.

For example, if DATA-1 has the value 100, then:

```
* Stores the value DATA-1 - 5, or 100 - 5, or 95,
* into DATA-2
  SUBTRACT 5 FROM DATA-1 GIVING DATA-2.
```

See also "Phrases" in this part for more information about the ROUNDED, ON SIZE ERROR, and CORRESPONDING phrases.

SUPPRESS

The SUPPRESS command stops the display of a report. The SUPPRESS command has the following format:

SUPPRESS PRINTING.

The SUPPRESS command can only be used within a procedure specified with the USE BEFORE REPORTING command. Even though the output of a report is suppressed, all LINE NUMBER and NEXT GROUP phrases are still performed, and the line counter is updated.

TERMINATE

The TERMINATE command ends the processing of a specified report. The TERMINATE command has the following format:

TERMINATE {report-name-1}...

When using the TERMINATE command, don't forget the following points:

✦ When the TERMINATE command is called, the report writer writes and displays all control footing groups in ascending order from the lowest level.

✦ If the TERMINATE command is called and the GENERATE command has not been called, no output will be produced.

✦ The TERMINATE command can't be executed for a report until the INITIATE command is executed.

✦ The TERMINATE command doesn't close any files associated with the report; this must be done separately using the CLOSE command.

✦ More than one report name can be specified.

You'll be back to look at this example of the TERMINATE command:

```
* Do the report thing...
  INITIATE REPORT-1.
  GENERATE REPORT-1.
  TERMINATE REPORT-1.
```

UNSTRING

The UNSTRING command separates one long data item into separate parts. (UNSTRING is the opposite of the STRING command.) The UNSTRING command has the following format:

```
UNSTRING identifier-1
   [DELIMITED BY [ALL]
      {identifier-2 or literal-1}
      [OR [ALL] {identifier-3 or literal-2}]...]
   INTO {identifier-4 [DELIMITER IN identifier-5]
      [COUNT IN identifier-6]}...
[WITH POINTER identifier-7]
[TALLYING IN identifier-8]
[ON OVERFLOW imperative-statement-1]
[NOT ON OVERFLOW imperative-statement-2]
[END-UNSTRING].
```

When using the UNSTRING command, remember the following things:

✦ Literal-1 and the literal-2 must be nonnumeric literals.

✦ Identifier-1, identifier-2, identifier-3, and identifier-5 must be alphanumeric data items.

✦ Identifier-4 must be an alphabetic item.

✦ Identifier-6 and identifier-8 must be integers.

✦ If the DELIMITED phrase is specified, it is followed by a character that delineates each item in identifier-1. Items are retrieved from identifier-1 and placed into the identifiers specified after the INTO phrase. If the DELIMITED phrase is not specified, each identifier specified after the INTO phrase is filled to its length before the next item is filled.

✦ If the TALLYING phrase is specified, the identifier specified will contain the number of items retrieved.

✦ If the OVERFLOW phrase is specified, the statement that follows will be executed if you have more characters in the data item, identifier-1, than can fit in the data items specified after the INTO phrase. If all the characters in the data item, identifier-1, are used, the statement following the NOT OVER-FLOW phrase is executed if it's included.

✦ If the POINTER phrase is specified, then characters are transferred from the data item, identifier-1, starting at the character position specified by identifier-7.

✦ If the COUNT phrase is specified for an destination data item, then it will contain the number of characters transferred into that destination data item.

The following example shows you the UNSTRING command in action:

```
* Type to cut the string loose
  UNSTRING MY-DATA
  DELIMITED BY "*"
    INTO DATA-1 DATA-2 DATA-3
    TALLYING COUNTER
  END-UNSTRING.
```

If MY-DATA contained *123*ABCDE*FUN WOW*, then after executing the UNSTRING command, DATA-1 would contain 123, DATA-2 would contain ABCDE, and DATA-3 would contain FUN WOW. The value in COUNTER would be 3, because three items were retrieved from MY-DATA.

USE

The USE command creates special handling routines that apply to debugging, file exception handling, and reporting. The USE command had the following four formats:

FORMAT 1:

```
USE [GLOBAL] AFTER STANDARD
{EXCEPTION or ERROR} PROCEDURE ON
{{file-name-1}... or INPUT or OUTPUT or I-O or EXTEND}.
```

FORMAT 2:

```
USE AFTER STANDARD

  {EXCEPTION or ERROR} PROCEDURE ON

  {{file-name-1}... or OUTPUT or EXTEND}.
```

FORMAT 3:

```
USE [GLOBAL] BEFORE REPORTING identifier-1.
```

FORMAT 4:

```
USE FOR DEBUGGING ON
  {cd-name-1 or
  [ALL REFERENCES OF] identifier-1 or file-name-1 or
    procedure-name-1 or ALL PROCEDURES}...
```

Formats 1, 2, and 4 of the USE command come up in debugging and exception handling. (**See also** Part IX for more information on debugging your COBOL programs.)

Format 3 of the USE command executes a procedure before reporting begins. The USE BEFORE REPORTING command can only appear in the declaratives section (*see also* Part IV for more information on the declaratives section). Identifier-1 specifies the report group, which when generated causes the procedure that follows the USE BEFORE REPORTING command to be executed. The GLOBAL phrase is new to the USE BEFORE REPORTING command. When you include the GLOBAL phrase, the procedure specified will be executed even if the report is executed from a nested program (*see also* Part I for more information on nesting programs).

Check out the following example of the USE BEFORE REPORTING command:

```
* Define The Procedure Division
  PROCEDURE DIVISION.
  DECLARATIVES.
     USE BEFORE REPORTING REPORT-1.
     REPORT-1-PRE-PROCESSING.
* Define REPORT-1 pre processing routine here
  END DECLARATIVES.
```

WRITE

The WRITE command writes a record to a specified position in a file or to position lines of text vertically on a page. The WRITE command has the following two formats:

FORMAT 1:

```
WRITE record-name-1 [FROM identifier-1]
  [{BEFORE or AFTER} ADVANCING
    {{identifier-2 or integer-1} [LINE or LINES] or
     {mnemonic-name-1 or
     PAGE}}]
[AT {END-OF-PAGE or EOP} imperative-statement-1]
[NOT AT {END-OF-PAGE or EOP} imperative-statement-2]
[INVALID KEY imperative-statement-1]
    [NOT INVALID KEY imperative-statement-2]
[END-WRITE].
```

FORMAT 2:

```
WRITE record-name-1 [FROM identifier-1]
[INVALID KEY imperative-statement-1]
[NOT INVALID KEY imperative-statement-2]
[END-WRITE].
```

When using Format 1 of the WRITE command, keep the following points in the back of your head:

+ Record-name-1 must be defined in the Data division and associated with an output or input-output file.

+ When a data item is specified in identifier-1, it can't be part of record-name-1.

+ Identifier-2 must be an integer item, and integer-1 can be zero. These values specify the number of line feeds to send before or after the record is written.

+ When the END-OF-PAGE or NOT END-OF-PAGE phrase is specified, the LINAGE clause must be included in the file description entry related to record-name-1. When the END OF PAGE or NOT END OF PAGE condition is true, the statement that follows is executed.

+ A WRITE command can't use both the ADVANCING PAGE phrase and END-OF-PAGE phrase.

+ The ADVANCING phrase, which specifies how many line feeds to send BEFORE or AFTER writing the current record, can only be used in a WRITE statement sending output to a file.

When using Format 2 of the WRITE command, remember the following things:

+ The record-name-1 must be the name of the record defined in the file section of the data division. The file must be open for output or input-output mode.

+ When a data item is specified in identifier-1, the same area must not be specified for record-name-1.

+ If an invalid key condition occurs during execution of the WRITE command, the command will fail. The record area of the file related to record-name-1 remains unchanged, and the statement following the INVALID KEY phrase is executed.

The following code shows you an example of the WRITE command which stores the data in RECORD-1 and performs some end of page logic:

```
* Write RECORD-1 and check for end of page
  WRITE RECORD-1
    AT END-OF-PAGE PERFORM PAGE-END-ROUTINE
  END-WRITE.
```

Part VII

Working with Files

Files are one of the most important aspects of COBOL applications. Many COBOL applications store and process data contained in files.

This part describes the different file types supported by COBOL and reviews their strengths and weaknesses, and explains how to implement each of these files types in your own COBOL applications.

In this part . . .

✔ **Getting to know your file basics**

✔ **Turning your keys into relative addresses**

✔ **Discovering I-O status**

✔ **Touching base with other file types**

Acquainting Yourself with File Organization

File organization is the way in which data records are stored on a file-storage device. You can use three primary methods of file organization in COBOL: index, relative, and sequential. COBOL also supports two other special types of files: report and sort-merge type files.

Index files

Index files represent something of a balance between sequential file organization and relative file organization. An index file allows sequential storage but also allows the same random accessing or processing of relative files.

Index files use an index table that indicates the approximate location for a given record. Unlike relative files, the key to address translation is built in.

An index file is more than just a single file. It's made up of two files, the main file and the index. The main file is where the data records are stored. The index file is used to randomly access records that are in the main file.

The index file functions similarly to a library card catalog. I know it's hard to remember these catalogs, but some libraries haven't completely computerized just yet. If you're trying to find a book by a particular author (for example, Asimov), you would look at the labels on the front of the drawers. These labels show the first few letters that the first card in the drawer begins with and the first few letters that the last card in the drawer begins with. You search for the drawer that would be in the same range as the name of the author who you're looking for (in this case, Asimov). After you open the drawer, you search sequentially until you find the first card where Asimov begins. After you find the card, it tells you exactly where to go to find that particular book.

Without the card index, you would be forced to search the entire library from top to bottom until you found the particular book you want — this could be quite a daunting task in a large library; you don't want to spend days looking for just one book. You may have an advantage of knowing where the types of books you're looking for are stored on the shelf, which could certainly help you to narrow your search. There may not have been room, though, for the book you're looking for in that particular area, and it may be stored in a completely different part of the library. Without the card index, you wouldn't have even known the book existed!

Index files work in the same way. When you want to access a key, such as Asimov, the index is searched until a record is found that equals or exceeds Asimov. At that point, you have found the group of records that includes the Asimov record. Each entry in the index files contains an address of the record in the main file. The index file is then searched until a matching record is found.

Index files are automatically created by the operating system, and slightly different indexing methods may be used on different platforms. When creating and using an index file, note that the key that identifies each record *must* be unique. So, using a key such as a customer's last name probably isn't a good idea when you have a number of customers with the last name of Smith or Johnson.

An index file is best illustrated by the following figure:

MAIN FILE		INDEX FILE	
RECORD ADDRESS	RECORD DATA	KEY	START ADDRESS
00	RECORD KEY 1234	1234	00
10	RECORD KEY 6134	6134	10
20	RECORD KEY 8125	8125	20

When records are deleted from an index file, they are normally tagged as deleted but aren't physically erased. This doesn't affect your programs, because deleted records are automatically skipped when you read the index file.

The CLOSE, DELETE, OPEN, READ, REWRITE, START, USE, and WRITE verbs can be used with index files. Index files can be accessed in sequential, random, and dynamic modes.

Relative files

A *relative file* is one in which records are accessed by reference to their relative position in the file. If a file contains 100 records, the first record in the file has a relative key of 1, and the last record has a relative key of 100.

A relative file can be read in a random order by simply using the relative key of each record. With a relative file, it's possible to give commands such as "Write a record as the 50th record in the file" or "Read the 98th record in the file." Records are retrieved using their relative addresses. An absolute address, on the other hand, would specify the disk volume, cylinder, track, and record number.

A relative file is best illustrated by the following figure:

RECORD KEY 1234	EMPTY	EMPTY	RECORD KEY 6134	RECORD KEY 8125	EMPTY	RECORD KEY 4377	EMPTY

Relative file organization is ideal in the case where records are identified by consecutive numbers. For instance, suppose that invoice records are numbered 0001, 0002, 0003, and so on. Relative organization can be used to store the records in the order of the invoice number. To access invoice 0050, you simply need to access the record whose relative key is 50.

However, records can rarely be consecutively numbered. More often, you need to use some indexing techniques to transform a record identifier into a relative record address.

A number of different methods can be used to transform record keys — or identifiers — into relative locations addresses. All the methods share one common attribute: They enable you to transform record keys, such as product numbers, social security numbers, customer numbers, and customer names, into relative key values.

For example, to retrieve a record for customer 1212, you apply the transformation method to obtain a relative key (for example, 99). You can then access the 99th record in the file to retrieve the record that contains the information for customer number 1212. (Algorithms for transforming record keys into relative addresses are described in "Transforming Keys into Relatives Addresses," later in this part.)

Because relative files allow you to access specific records directly, they can provide a very high level of performance. However, the level of performance is very dependent on the record keys that are chosen and the transformation method that is used. You now have a chance to become a mad scientist, because this process requires a bit of experimentation to find the combination that works best for your application.

The big reason for the variability in performance is due to duplicates. All key-to-address transformation methods produce duplicate relative address values when given different record keys. How often these duplicates are produced is the primary cause for performance differences. Again, it's important to realize that all methods produce duplicate relative addresses at some time. You must have a methodology for handling these duplicate relative addresses.

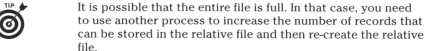
You can handle duplicate relative addresses in a number of ways. The most successful way is to use the following process when writing records:

1. When a file is created, use a special field in each record to indicate its current status; mark each record as being empty.

2. As a new record is written, use the chosen key-to-address transformation to obtain the relative address.

3. Read the record that is currently stored at the relative address.

4. If the record is marked as empty, then everything is cool. You can write the new record and mark the record as filled.

5. If the record is marked as filled, continue reading records sequentially, starting at the next record, until an empty record is found. If the end of the file is reached while reading records sequentially, begin again by starting at the first record.

It is possible that the entire file is full. In that case, you need to use another process to increase the number of records that can be stored in the relative file and then re-create the relative file.

That takes care of writing records, but you also need to take special actions when reading records. The following process is required when reading records:

1. Use the chosen key-to-address transformation method to obtain the relative address.

2. Read the record at the relative address.

3. If the record is marked as empty, then the record does not exist.

4. If the record is not marked as empty, compare the key of the record read to the record key that you want. If they are equal, you have read the correct record.

5. If the key that you are searching for and the key of the record read are not equal, continue reading records sequentially until you find the record that you're searching for or find an empty record. If you find an empty record first, you can conclude that the record you're searching for does not exist. If the end of the file is encountered while reading records sequentially, resume your search at the beginning of the file.

If the entire file is full, the worst-case scenario is that you may read the entire file sequentially and still not find your record.

Finally, if you can delete records from your file, the methods that are used when reading and writing the file must be modified. First, whenever you delete a record from the file, the record's status should be changed from filled to deleted. Whenever you write a new record, a deleted-record status is equivalent to an empty-record status. However, when you read a record, deleted records should not be considered the same as empty records. The deleted record could have been present when the records that you were searching for were added to the file.

The CLOSE, DELETE, OPEN, READ, REWRITE, START, USE, and WRITE verbs can be used with relative files. Relative files can be accessed in sequential, random, and dynamic modes.

Report files

A report file is a sequential output file that is defined using the REPORT clause. This type of file consists of records that are written by the Report Writer Control System. A report file doesn't define any specific records. It can only have the OPEN, CLOSE, GENERATE, INITIATE, SUPPRESS, TERMINATE, USE BEFORE REPORTING, and USE AFTER EXCEPTION statements executed on it.

Sequential files

In a *sequential file,* the records are written in a serial order and are read in the same order as they are written. The serial order doesn't need to be in a particular sequence, such as according to account number.

In legacy applications, files that are assigned to a card reader, printer, and magnetic tape drive are always organized as sequential files. Files that are stored on disks and other direct-access storage devices can be sequential, index-sequential, or relative files.

A sequential file is best illustrated by the following figure:

RECORD-1	RECORD-2	RECORD-3	......	RECORD-N

Sequential files that are stored on tape or disk are usually sorted so that the records are in a logical sequential order. For example, in a file containing employee information, the records may be sorted using the employee identification number. The SORT command is used to order files based on key values.

The practice of sorting records in a specific order is helpful for batch-oriented applications, where a file is read from beginning to end, and some operation is performed. When new records are added to a sequential file, they are added at the end of the file.

To reorder a sequential file after adding records, the SORT command must be called. Depending on the size of the file, the sort could take a considerable amount of time. If your applications require data to be accessed in a sorted order — and your data file is updated often — you should consider using index-type files instead. Index file types provide the best attributes of direct access and sequential processing — allowing records to be read in random order as well as in a sequentially-sorted order. The sorting of an index file happens without having to explicitly sort the file.

The CLOSE, OPEN, READ, REWRITE, USE, and WRITE verbs can be used with sequential files. Note that the only file-access mode that can be used with sequential files is the sequential mode.

Sort-merge files

A sort file contains a collection of records that are to be sorted. This type of file is created when — not surprisingly — you call the SORT command. The sort file is used as a temporary storage area; it can't be accessed outside of the SORT command. Sort files are specified by a file control entry, and their layout is specified by a sort-merge file description.

Transforming Keys into Relative Addresses

Four commonly used methods can transform record keys into relative addresses: alphabetic keys, division-remainder, folding, and mid-square. Although other methods can be used when accessing relative files, these four are the most common. Each methodology has its own strengths and weaknesses, and each may only be applicable with certain types of keys.

Alphabetic keys

What happens when your key just isn't numeric? Well, first you must convert the alphabetic key into a numeric value. A common way to convert a key into a number is to use a simple substitution method (for example, A = 00, B = 01, C = 02, and so on). Using this method, a key such as MARIE would become 1200170804. After you convert the alphabetic key into a numeric value, you can use any of the key transformation methods such as division-remainder, folding, or the mid-square method.

Division-remainder method

When using the division-remainder method, you must first choose the number of records that are to be stored in the file. When determining the file size, a good rule of thumb is to divide the desired number of records by 0.80. The records that you want to store will occupy 80 percent of the file size, and the remaining 20 percent will be slack space. This slack space reduces the number of duplicate relative key address values.

After the file size has been determined, you need to determine the prime number that's closest to the file size. For example, to create a relative file to store 9,600 records that are identified by a six-digit key value, you would compute the file size needed by dividing 9,600 by 0.80; this equals 12,000 records. The prime number closest to 12,000 is 11,987.

There are a number of methods available to help you determine if a number is prime or not. One of the most popular methods is the Sieve of Eratosthenes — discovered in 240 BC. The Sieve algorithm is pretty basic; you just make a list of numbers less than or equal to the number you're searching for, and cross out the multiples of all primes less than or equal to the square root of the number you're looking for; all the numbers remaining are prime.

You may also want to check out the Web site www.utm.edu/research/primes/notes/100000.txt, which lists the first 100,000 prime numbers.

To determine the relative address for a key, follow these steps:

1. Divide the record key value by the prime number. If your key value is 987654, then you divide 987,654 by 11,987 to produce a quotient of 82 and a remainder of 4,720.

2. Add 1 to the remainder to produce the relative key address. In this example, the relative key address would be 4721.

The division-remainder method is one of the easiest methods to apply, and it produces a good distribution of keys, resulting in few duplicates. The following example demonstrates how the division-remainder method could be implemented in your COBOL application:

```
MOVE KEY-VALUE OF CUST-RECORD TO WORK-KEY
DIVIDE PRIME-NUMBER INTO WORK-KEY GIVING QUOTIENT
COMPUTE RELATIVE-ADDRESS = WORK-KEY - (PRIME-NUMBER * QUOTIENT)
    + 1
```

The division-remainder method only works on numeric key values.

Folding method

When using the folding method, the key is separated into two parts, which are then added to form the address. For example, to convert the key 87654321 into a four-digit relative address, you could take the first four digits and add the last three digits to produce a new four-digit key, using only the last four digits of the result as the key; in this example, 8765 + 321 = 9086. If the result of your addition is greater than four digits, only use the last four of the result. For example: if your key is 9765999, then 9765+999 = 10764. Truncating to just use the last four digits, your key will be 0764.

You can also fold digits in other ways. Try all kinds of combinations; for example, (a) add the first four digits to the last four digits or (b) use the middle four digits, add the first two digits, and then add the last two digits. As with all the key transformation methods, your mileage may vary — you need to experiment to find the methods that are most appropriate for your application.

The folding method only works when you are using numeric key values.

Mid-square method

When using the mid-square key transformation method, the key is multiplied by itself — or squared. The relative address is then computed by using the appropriate number of digits from the middle of the result. For example, to convert the key 52566 into a four-digit relative address, you would square 52,566 to produce the result 2,763,184,356. You would then use the middle four digits of the result, 3184, as your relative address.

The mid-square method only works when you are using numeric key values.

Using I-O Status

I-O status is a two-character code that indicates the status of file operations. An I-O status data element is created by using the FILE STATUS directive when specifying file control information in the ENVIRONMENT DIVISION.

In previous versions of the COBOL standard, the left-most character of the I-O status was called status key 1 and the right-most character was called status key 2. In the ANSI-85 standard, this distinction can no longer be made.

The following table clarifies I-O status keys:

I-O Status First Digit	Indicates This
0	Successful completion
1	At-end condition
2	Invalid key
3	Permanent error
4	Error in application logic
9	Platform-specific error

The common I-O status values are described in the following table. An X in the Sequential, Relative, or Index columns indicates that the status value can be returned by the file type.

Value	Meaning	Sequential	Relative	Index
00	Operation was completed successfully	X	X	X
02	Duplicate key detected for READ, REWRITE, or WRITE	-	-	X
04	Length mismatch between record and its description during a READ operation	X	X	X
05	OPEN performed for an optional file that was not present	X	X	X
07	CLOSE with reel option done on a non-reel-type file	X	-	-
10	At-end condition encountered during a sequential READ operation or an optional input file was not present	X	X	X
14	Relative record number has more digits than record key when performing a sequential READ operation	-	X	-
21	Sequence error occurred when sequentially accessing an index file	-	X	-
22	Attempted to WRITE a record with a duplicate key	-	-	X
23	Attempted to access a nonexistent record, or attempted to START or READ an optional file that is not present	-	X	X

Value	Meaning	Sequential	Relative	Index
24	Attempted to WRITE beyond file boundaries	-	X	X
30	Permanent error — no further information is available	X	X	X
34	Boundary violation occurred, typically because a record was too large	X	-	-
35	Attempted to OPEN a nonoptional file that is not present	X	X	X
37	Attempted to OPEN a file in a mode that is not compatible with the type of the file (for example, when trying to open a sequential file in an index or relative mode)	X	X	X
38	Attempted to OPEN a file that is currently locked	X	X	X
39	Failure occurred during an OPEN operation due to a file attribute conflict	X	X	X
41	Attempted to OPEN a file that was already opened	X	X	X
42	Attempted to CLOSE a file that is not open	X	X	X
43	Attempted to DELETE or REWRITE before a successful READ of the record was performed	X	X	X
44	Boundary violation occurred because of a WRITE or REWRITE with an incorrect record size, or for sequential files, the record was not the same size as the one being replaced	X	X	X
46	Sequential READ was attempted, but the end of file has already been reached	X	X	X
47	Attempted to READ or START a file that was not open in input or I-O mode	X	X	X
48	Attempted to WRITE to a file that was not open in output, I-O, or extend mode	X	X	X
49	Attempted to REWRITE or DELETE a file that was not open in I-O mode	X	X	X

(continued)

Value	Meaning	Sequential	Relative	Index
9x	Codes reserved for platform- or compiler-specific errors. Consult your COBOL compiler-specific documentation for further information on these error codes.	X	X	X

To develop the most robust applications, it's important to check the I-O status after every file operation. The following example demonstrates how to check the I-O status:

```
IDENTIFICATION DIVISION.
PROGRAM-ID.  CHECK-FILE-STATUS.
ENVIRONMENT DIVISION.
INPUT-OUTPUT SECTION.
FILE-CONTROL.
   SELECT MY-FILE ASSIGN TO MY-MASTER-FILE
   FILE STATUS IS MASTER-IO-STATUS
.
.
DATA DIVISION.
.
.
WORKING-STORAGE SECTION.
   01  MASTER-IO-STATUS      PIC X(2).
.
.
PROCEDURE DIVISION.
.
.
   OPEN INPUT MASTERFILE
   IF MASTER-IO-STATUS NOT EQUAL TO "00"
   DISPLAY "File status error returned on OPEN - " MASTER-IO-
      STATUS
.
```

Part VIII

The Flowchart Reference

I know what you're thinking — *flowcharting!?* Didn't that go out the door with punch cards? In many cases it did. But what if you're working on a legacy application that was developed years ago?

In many cases, the most useful and understandable documentation that you have is a flowchart. Flowcharts can help you understand the structure and flow of your COBOL applications. One of the hardest tasks any programmer can take on is understanding a program written by someone else. Understanding flowcharts — if they're available — can be an important tool in the programmer's tool box.

It may have been some time — if ever — since you have seen a flowchart. Flowcharts are a way to describe and analyze processes. They help you break down a complex process (like making your morning cup of coffee) into logical steps, and they let you display a process in an easy-to-understand visual manner. In this part, you identify flowcharting symbols, interpret program flowcharts, and find tools that can turn this whole task into an automated process.

In this part . . .

✔ **Identifying flowchart symbols**

✔ **Interpreting program flowcharts**

✔ **Using tools to automatically generate flowcharts**

✔ **Finding more information on flowcharts**

Flowcharting Symbols

Just like a map uses symbols to represent rest stops, highways, and mountains, flowcharts also use a number of different symbols to represent key items. The key to understanding flowcharts is understanding what each of the symbols looks like and means.

A number of ANSI-recognized flowcharting symbols appear in standard flowcharts. The following table shows the 27 most commonly used programming-related symbols.

Symbol	What It's Called	What It Does
	Alternate Process	This process-type symbol usually represents an event that occurs automatically — such as an end-of-file condition.
	Card	This is a blast from the past — punch cards. The symbol indicates that some data or other information is read from a stack of punch cards. Hopefully, the cards are in the right order — or you have a mess on your hands.
	Collate	This symbol typically indicates the sorting of a file in alphabetical order.
	Connector	Arrows usually connect one part of a flowchart to another. Sometimes, though, it's just not practical to draw a mile-long line to connect two points. That's where connectors come in. You use connectors in pairs: Draw an arrow to a connector, give the connector a name, and where the arrow should really go, place a connector nearby. Give the connector the same name and draw an arrow coming out to where the line would actually go.
⟶	Data or Process Flow	Like pipes in your house that direct water to your kitchen sink, data or process flow in a flowchart is represented by arrows. Just connect the dots — follow the arrows to work through the process that's depicted by the flowchart.

Symbol	What It's Called	What It Does
	Data	This symbol usually indicates a data input or output operation.
	Decision	Why are there so many questions? A decision symbol asks a question and follows a certain path depending on the answer. A decision symbol typically represents a logical expression that has a Yes/No or True/False answer.
	Delay	Take it easy; have a cup of java. This symbol means to wait for a specified period of time or for another event or process to be completed.
	Direct Access Storage	This symbol identifies a direct-access file, which is typically an indexed file. Usually this type of information is stored on a disk drive, which in previous days looked like the drum of a washing machine. That explains why the symbol looks like a cylinder that got knocked over.
	Display	This symbol means to send output to a terminal, window, or form.
	Document	This symbol refers to an external document that provides more detailed information.
	Extract	Extract usually identifies a process where certain records in a file are retrieved.
	Internal Storage	This symbol identifies a local variable or internal program storage.
	Magnetic Disk	This symbol identifies storage with an engaging personality. You may be familiar with magnetic disks today, but in the past, they were very expensive — data was often stored on a tape or card deck because it was cheaper to do so.
	Manual Input	This symbol tells the program to wait for someone to feed the program some information from a keyboard or terminal.

(continued)

Symbol	What It's Called	What It Does
	Manual Operation	Even the best-laid plans require a little nudge now and then. This symbol indicates an operation that occurs through manual intervention.
	Merge	Sometimes you need to combine the contents of two files — just like running a mail merge with your word processor and a data file. The merge symbol indicates that two or more files are combined.
	Multi-Document	This symbol refers to some external documents which provide more detailed information.
	Off-Page Connector	Off-page connectors function in the same way as the connector symbol, except that the connection point is found on another page. Sometimes off-page connectors get pretty big — they just can't fit on a single page unless you're using tiny print.
	Predefined Process	A predefined process identifies a subroutine or procedure that performs a series of complex steps. This type of process usually has another associated flowchart that defines the step-by-step procedures it performs.
	Preparation	All good recipes require a bit of preparation — like heating the oven to 350 degrees before baking. The preparation symbol indicates a process or event that must be completed before the program is executed.
	Process	A process identifies a step or an action — such as read something from a file or set a variable to a value.
	Punched Tape	Wow — this is really old stuff! A really cheap way to store data in the past was to use punched tape. This type of media fell between punch cards and magnetic tape. A punched tape is a paper tape with holes in it that identifies data. This type of data storage is rarely used today.

Symbol	What It's Called	What It Does
	Sequential Access Storage	This symbol identifies a sequential file or device. In days gone by, this may have been a tape drive (which explains why the symbol looks somewhat like a reel-to-reel tape); today, this is typically a sequential file.
	Sort	You must have things in order! This symbol usually refers to the sorting of a file in some ordered manner.
	Stored Data	This symbol indicates that data is stored in a temporary location or file.
	Terminator	I'm not talking about Arnold here. A terminator identifies the beginning or end of a process. The terminator symbols are usually the first and last symbols of a flowchart. These symbols are somewhat like treasure-map symbols — begin here, and X marks the spot.

The following flowchart illustrates a simple application that reads and processes a file:

1. Open the Customer information file.

2. Open the Report output file.

3. Read the next record.

4. If the Customer State is New York (NY), go to write customer information; otherwise, go to end of file processing.

5. Write the customer information to the Report output file.

6. If the end of file has not been encountered, go to Read the next record; otherwise continue.

7. Close the Customer information file.

8. Close the Report output file.

After you understand what each of the symbols means, it's not hard to interpret a complete flowchart.

Outsourcing Flowcharts

If you find flowcharts a useful way to understand your existing COBOL applications, but you don't want to waste the time drawing the stuff by hand, a few companies can produce flowcharts and other documentation using your COBOL programs as input.

The following list details the names and addresses of companies I recommend:

✦ **CyberMetrics:** 5541 South Marine Drive, Tempe, AZ, 85251. Phone: 602-838-3310. Web site: www.cybermetrics.com

◆ **ReGenisys:** 4725 North Scottsdale Road, Suite 210, Scottsdale, AZ, 85251. Phone: 602-0970-1131. Web site: www.regenisys.com

◆ **Soft-Tek International:** 199 North Amidon, Wichita, KS, 67203. Phone: 316-838-7200. Web site: www.soft-tek.com

◆ **Viasoft:** 3033 North 44th Street, Phoenix, AZ, 85018. Phone: 602-952-0057. Web site: www.viasoft.com/main.htm

Surfing the Web for Flowcharting Information

If you're interested in even more flowcharting information, check out the following Web sites to satisfy your flowcharting cravings:

◆ **Flowcharts Central** (www.flowcharts.com/about_flow.html): Provides a complete reference to everything flowcharting.

◆ **Yahoo's List of Graphic Software Companies** (www.yahoo.com/Business_and_Economy/Companies/Computers/Software/Graphics): Provides a list of companies which provide flowcharting software.

Part IX

Debugging Your Applications

Debugging programs is just about as much fun as cleaning out your freezer. But, like death and taxes, you can't avoid debugging. Even if you're the most careful and consistent programmer, at some point, you need to debug your COBOL programs.

Debugging occurs at two levels when developing programs in any language: syntax and logical debugging. Fortunately, COBOL provides a number of features that help you debug your programs. These features include indicating debugging lines with a D in column 7, the USE FOR DEBUGGING command, and the USE AFTER EXCEPTION command. Compiler- and system-specific features can also help you debug your COBOL applications. These features include using the output of your COBOL compiler to find syntax errors and on-line system debuggers.

In this part . . .

✔ Uncovering logical errors in your COBOL programs

✔ Using program directives to debug your programs

✔ Stomping out syntax errors in you COBOL programs

✔ Breaking out the system debugger

Debugging Your Programs for Logical Errors

Logical errors are complicated to find and diagnose. These errors occur when your program is running and doesn't do what you intended it to do, or, if you're really unlucky, logical errors can cause your program to crash (stop running) before it reaches the end of the file.

It may not be possible to find logical errors during development time. Logically debugging your program should be part of an overall plan of testing, where you run your program with different types of input.

Fortunately, COBOL provides a number of features to assist you with the logical debugging of your program.

D directive

In the layout of COBOL source programs, all new paragraph names must begin in Area A (columns 8 through 11), and all the remaining source code appears in Area B (column 12 through the end of the line). *See also* Part I for more information on the layout of COBOL source programs.

Column 7 is a special area called the *indicator area,* which can have a special debugging directive if it contains a D — the D directive. The following example demonstrates the D directive:

```
* Display The Value Of X When In Debugging Mode
D DISPLAY "The Value Of X Is ", X
```

Debugging lines are only compiled into your program when you use the WITH DEBUGGING MODE directive in the ENVIRONMENT DIVISION (*see also* Part III for more information on the ENVI- RONMENT DIVISION). If you omit this directive, the debugging lines don't appear in the program.

Your application can't compile if the debugging lines aren't syntactically and logically correct.

One of the easiest ways to debug your programs for logical errors is to output the current value of a value or location in your program using the DISPLAY command (*see also* Part VI for more information on the DISPLAY command). It can be useful to output the current state of your program to the screen or a separate file to help you understand the flow of the program when something is going wrong. Including this type of output on debugging lines allows you to easily include debugging display information during development time and then turn it off when your program is correct and ready to move into production mode.

DEBUGGING MODE directive

The DEBUGGING MODE directive is a compile-time switch that determines whether debugging lines and USE FOR DEBUGGING statements are compiled. This directive is part of the SOURCE-COMPUTER directive in the ENVIRONMENT DIVISION, and it has the following format:

```
[SOURCE-COMPUTER. [computer-name
    [WITH DEBUGGING MODE].]]
```

If the DEBUGGING MODE is specified, or if the program is nested within a program that contains the DEBUGGING MODE clause, all debugging lines and USE FOR DEBUGGING statements are compiled into your program. (*See also* Part I for detailed information on nesting programs.) Debugging sections are only valid in your main program; they aren't valid in nested programs.

If DEBUGGING MODE is not specified, all debugging lines and USE FOR DEBUGGING statements are treated as comments.

DEBUG-ITEM area

Whenever a section that contains a USE FOR DEBUGGING statement is executed, a special information area, called a DEBUG-ITEM, is filled with information about what caused the execution of the debugging section.

The DEBUG-ITEM has the following description (you don't have to define the DEBUG-ITEM; the COBOL system creates it for you):

```
01DEBUG-ITEM.
   02 DEBUG-LINE     PIC X(6).
   02 FILLER         PIC X VALUE SPACE.
   02 DEBUG-NAME     PIC X(30).
   02 FILLER         PIC X VALUE SPACE.
   02 DEBUG-SUB-1    PIC S9999 SIGN IS LEADING SEPARATE CHARAC-
      TER.
   02 FILLER         PIC X VALUE SPACE.
   02DEBUG-SUB-2     PIC S9999 SIGN LEADING SEPARATE CHARACTER.
   02 FILLER         PIC X VALUE SPACE.
   02 DEBUG-SUB-3    PIC S9999 SIGN LEADING SEPARATE CHARACTER.
   02 FILLER         PICX VALUE SPACE.
   02 DEBUG-CONTENTS    PIC    X(n).
```

DEBUG-LINE contains a system-defined way of identifying the source statement; typically, its value would be a sequence number if sequence numbers are defined.

DEBUG-NAME contains the first 30 characters of the name that's defined in the USE FOR DEBUGGING statement. If the name defined is a table, then DEBUG-SUB-1, DEBUG-SUB-2, and DEBUG-SUB-3 contain the multiple sub-scripts that are currently in use by the table.

DEBUG-CONTENTS contains the contents of the item that is
specified in the USE FOR DEBUGGING statement.

USE AFTER EXCEPTION statement

USE AFTER EXCEPTION provides more than just a way to debug
your COBOL programs — it gives you a way to prevent and control
errors when they occur. The USE AFTER EXCEPTION statement
identifies a procedure that is called after an exception occurs
when referencing a file.

The USE AFTER EXCEPTION and ERROR statements are equivalent, and they have the following form:

```
USE AFTER STANDARD
     {EXCEPTION or ERROR} PROCEDURE ON
     {{file-name-1}... or OUTPUT or EXTEND}
```

To get the most benefit from the USE AFTER EXCEPTION statement, use it with the I-O status identifier. *See also* Part V for
more information on I-O status.

The USE AFTER EXCEPTION statement can only be used in the
declarative section of the PROCEDURE DIVISION (*see also* Part V
for more information on the PROCEDURE DIVISION declaratives
section), and only one USE AFTER EXCEPTION statement can be
used. This statement is followed by several procedure names that
define USE AFTER EXCEPTION procedures. If you attempt to
include a USE AFTER EXCEPTION statement anywhere besides
the declarative section of the PROCEDURE DIVISION, a syntax
error will result.

USE FOR DEBUGGING statement

The USE FOR DEBUGGING statement identifies an item or items
that are monitored by a debugging procedure. Whenever the item
identified in the USE FOR DEBUGGING statement is referenced,
the DEBUG-ITEM area is filled with the appropriate information.

The USE FOR DEBUGGING statement must appear in the PROCE-
DURE DIVISION and has the following format:

```
USE FOR DEBUGGING ON
     {cd-name-1 or
      [ALL REFERENCES OF] identifier-1 or file-name-1 or
      procedure-name-1 or ALL PROCEDURES}...
```

If *cd-name-1,* a communication device, is specified, the DEBUG-
ITEM is filled with information after the execution of any ENABLE,
DISABLE, SEND, or ACCEPT MESSAGE COUNT statement that
references the communications device, or after a RECEIVE
statement that references the communications device statement
is executed. The DEBUG-ITEM is updated as follows:

◆ DEBUG-LINE identifies the source statement that references the communications device.

◆ DEBUG-NAME contains the name of the communications device.

◆ DEBUG-CONTENTS contains the area that is associated with the communications device.

If *identifier-1,* any identifier, is specified, the DEBUG-ITEM is filled with information after any WRITE, REWRITE, PERFORM, MOVE, or GO TO with a DEPENDING ON phrase is executed that references the identifier. The DEBUG-ITEM is updated as follows:

◆ DEBUG-LINE identifies the source statement that references the identifier.

◆ DEBUG-NAME contains the name of the identifier.

◆ DEBUG-CONTENTS contains the contents of the identifier.

If *file-name-1,* any filename, is specified, the DEBUG-ITEM is filled with information after the execution of any OPEN, CLOSE, DELETE, or START statement that references the filename. The DEBUG-ITEM is updated as follows:

◆ DEBUG-LINE identifies the source statement that references the file name.

◆ DEBUG-NAME contains the filename.

◆ DEBUG-CONTENTS contains the entire record read if a READ statement was executed; otherwise it is blank.

If *procedure-name-1,* any procedure name, is specified, the DEBUG-ITEM is filled with information after the procedure is called in any way. The DEBUG-ITEM is updated as follows:

◆ DEBUG-LINE identifies the source statement that references the called procedure.

◆ DEBUG-NAME contains the name of the procedure.

◆ DEBUG-CONTENTS contains a string that identifies the current action that referenced the procedure.

If ALL PROCEDURES is specified, the DEBUG-ITEM is filled with information after the procedure is called in any way.

The DEBUG-ITEM is updated as follows:

◆ DEBUG-LINE identifies the source statement that references the called procedure.

◆ DEBUG-NAME contains the name of the procedure.

✦ DEBUG-CONTENTS contains a string that identifies the current action that referenced the procedure.

Debugging Your Programs for Syntax Errors

A syntax error usually occurs when you mistype something in your program's source code or when you just don't understand how a statement or command is used.

Acquainting yourself with the compiler

The purpose of a COBOL compiler is to take a program that is written using the COBOL programming language and produce a program that can be run on your system. Contrary to public opinion, computers are really stupid, and compilers are the best example of this fact. If you enter one small error in your program, from a missing period to a misspelled word, the compiler chokes and spits out an error message. Your program must be absolutely perfect — from a syntax point of view — before it can be compiled.

Interpreting the compilation output

When you compile your COBOL programs, the compiler produces some type of output to tell you if any syntax errors were found. The output of your compiler and its format vary widely from one compiler to another. It's important to understand what your compiler is trying to tell you. You can then understand how and where to fix your program so that it can compile correctly.

To help you understand the output of your COBOL compiler, review the following example program, which intentionally contains a few syntax errors:

```
01      IDENTIFICATION DIVISION
02      PROGRAM-ID. HELLOAPP.
03
04      DATA DIVISION.
05      WORKING-STORAGE SECTION.
06
07      01 PROGRAM-WORK-FIELDS.
08          05 INPUT-NAME       PIS X(30).
09          05 OUTPUT-NAME      PIC X(37).
10
11      01 PROGRAM-FLAGS.
12          05 LOOP-FLAG        PIC 9(1).
13              88 LOOP-DONE     VALUE 1.
14
15      PROCEDURE DIVISION.
16
```

```
17              INITIALIZE PROGRAM-WORK-FIELDS
18                        PROGRAM-FLAGS.
19
20              PERFORM UNTIL LOOP-DONE
21                  DISPLAY " "
22                  DISPLAY "ENTER A NAME OR Q TO QUIT:"
23                  ACCEPT INPUT-NAME
24                  IF FUNCTION UPPER-CASE(INPUT-NAME) = "Q"
25                      SET LOOP-DONE TO TRUE
26                  ELSE
27                      MOVE SPACES TO OUTPUT-NAME
28                      MOVE "HELLO, TO OUTPUT-NAME (1:7)
29                      MOVE INPUT-NAME TO OUTPUT-NAME (8:30)
30                      DISPLAY OUTPUT-NAME
31                  END-IF
32              END PERFORM.
```

This program contains the following errors:

+ On line 01, a period is missing after the IDENTIFICATION DIVISION header.

+ On line 08, the PIC directive is misspelled as *PIS*.

+ The from literal HELLO, specified in the MOVE command on line 28, is missing the closing quotation mark.

+ On line 32, the END-PERFORM directive is misspelled as END PERFORM (the hyphen is missing).

These are fairly simple errors that can and do commonly occur in all programs at some time.

This program produces a number of errors when you attempt to compile it. Even though there are only four errors in the program, your compiler may tell you that there are more. When a compiler encounters an error, it may not be able to pinpoint where the error is. Sometimes, the compiler needs to read a bit farther ahead in the code before it can find something that it recognizes again.

While compiler outputs vary greatly, they are relatively easy to interpret. Start with the first error and work your way through. The situation is usually not as bad as it looks, because multiple errors can often be traced back to a single problem.

When your COBOL compiler encounters a syntax error, the compiler usually reports a line number where the error was found, and it shows a descriptive message. Sometimes the line number is slightly off, so you may need to look back a few lines to find the error.

When attempting to compile the previous error-riddled program using the IBM VisualAge COBOL compiler, the following output was produced. (Remember, the output of your COBOL compiler may look different.)

```
IBM(R) Program Maintenance Utility for Windows(R)
Version 3.50.000 Feb 13 1996
Copyright (C) IBM Corporation 1988-1995
Copyright (C) Microsoft Corp. 1988-1991
All rights reserved.

" Compile "
 rexx.exe IWZVCOMP.CMD -Q"EXIT(ADEXIT(IWZRMGUX)) ADATA" -
    COMPRC_OK=4 C:\HELLOAPP\HELLOAPP.CBL HELLOAPP.EXE
Starting COBOL compile of C:\HELLOAPP\HELLOAPP.CBL ...


c:\helloapp\helloapp.cbl(2:8) : IGYDS1082-E: A period was
        required.  A period was assumed before "PROGRAM-ID".
c:\helloapp\helloapp.cbl(8:8) : IGYDS1089-S: "PIS" was
        invalid.  Scanning was resumed at the next area "A"
        item, level-number, or the start of the next clause.
c:\helloapp\helloapp.cbl(8:8) : IGYDS1159-E: A "PICTURE"
        clause was not found for elementary item "INPUT-NAME".
        "PICTURE X(1)" was assumed.
c:\helloapp\helloapp.cbl(20:8) : IGYPS2112-E: The
        "PERFORM" verb did not have a matching scope
        terminator.  A scope terminator was inserted on line
        34.  The execution results may not be correct.
c:\helloapp\helloapp.cbl(29:8) : IGYPS0007-E: A
        nonnumeric literal was not properly continued.  The end
        of the literal was assumed on the last source line.
c:\helloapp\helloapp.cbl(29:8) : IGYPS0088-S: The "MOVE"
        statement was invalid.  Expected "TO", but found
        "MOVE".  The statement was discarded.
c:\helloapp\helloapp.cbl(32:8) : IGYPS2112-E: The
        "PERFORM" verb did not have a matching scope
        terminator.  A scope terminator was inserted on line
        34.  The execution results may not be correct.
c:\helloapp\helloapp.cbl(32:8) : IGYPS2072-S: "END" was
        invalid.  Skipped to the next verb, period or
        procedure-name definition.

igyccob2 -q"exit(adexit(iwzrmgux)) adata" -q"noterminal"
    c:\helloapp\helloapp.cbl
COBOL compile complete, return code = 12
Processing halted.
NMAKE : fatal error U1077: 'rexx.exe' : return code '12'
Stop.
```

For each error encountered, the line number is reported first, followed by a descriptive error message. As I previously mentioned, the line number can be slightly off. For example, the first error message reports an error on line 02, but the error is actually caused by a missing period on line 01.

Because the output of each COBOL compiler varies, you need to consult the documentation that's included with your COBOL compiler to help you interpret any output that is produced by the compiler. Some compilers also report specific error numbers, which are also referenced in your compiler-specific documentation.

Sometimes you go through and fix all the errors reported by your compiler, and then you recompile the program, only to get another list of errors. Cool down — this is a common occurrence and can be caused by the following items:

+ You may not have fixed the error in the first place — make sure you go back through the source code and error list to assure you haven't missed anything. It doesn't take much, even a missing period, to throw a monkey wrench in the whole process.

+ The compiler may have encountered too many errors. If this happens, the compiler may decide to throw in the towel and stop processing your program. After you fix the first set of errors, the compiler can process more of your program and find errors that occur after the errors that you first fixed.

Some COBOL compilers come as part of a complete development environment, which includes *intelligent editors*. Many of these head-of-the-class editors can identify some of the basic syntax errors before you attempt to compile your application, preventing you from wasting time in correcting simple programming errors. Examples include The MicroFocus and IBM VisualAge COBOL development environments.

Using Your System Debugger

Almost every COBOL development system that you encounter works with or provides a system-level debugger that allows you to locate logical bugs and analyze the behavior of your programs.

The features that are provided by system-level debuggers vary widely from platform to platform. Some of the more full-featured debuggers, such as Xpeditor in the MVS environment or the debugger included with IBM VisualAge for COBOL, allow you to do the following tasks:

+ Watch your source code execute line by line

+ Control the execution of your program line by line

+ Watch the contents of certain data items change as your program executes

✦ Cause your program to stop at a specific line or whenever a specific variable or procedure is referenced

Consult the documentation that is included with your compiler and your system to determine the specific features that are provided by your system debugger. Your compiler may also require you to specify special directives to enable debugging; again, consult your compiler documentation.

Part X

Compiler Considerations and CICS

The COBOL programming language has a long history, and, not surprisingly, COBOL is supported on a wide range of hardware platforms — from mainframes to mid-range systems to PCs.

While this book focuses on the ANSI-85 COBOL standard language, a number of different versions of COBOL are designed to take advantage of platform-specific features, such as CICS (Customer Information Control System) on IBM mainframes and midrange systems. (CICS is IBM's on-line transaction processing environment.) CICS provides COBOL applications with the ability to create interactive user interfaces that handle very large transaction volumes with fast response times.

In this part . . .

✔ **Using COBOL with your Web server**

✔ **Adding object oriented programming features to COBOL**

✔ **Calling CICS from COBOL — an introduction**

Considering COBOL Compilers

With the rate of change in the computer industry, you may think that a programming language with such a long history could be near the end of its usefulness. Nothing could be further from the truth when it comes to COBOL. COBOL continues to evolve and remains a viable programming language today, including support for COBOL as a language for development of Internet applications and the addition of object-oriented programming features into the COBOL programming language.

COBOL on the Internet

You may be surprised to discover that COBOL, one of the oldest programming languages, has found a home in the fast paced world of Internet development.

To keep their products on the cutting edge of the Internet, many COBOL compiler manufacturers now provide support for creating COBOL applications that can be used on the Internet. For example, common gateway interfaces (CGI) are programs that are executed by a Web server when they are called by client browsers. CGI programs are used to provide an interface to system applications and resources. One of the most typical uses of CGI applications is to process information returned when filling out a Web page form.

Depending on your compiler and system, COBOL programs can be used as CGI programs by calling them indirectly from other CGI-enabled programming languages such as C or C++. Some COBOL compilers (such as the MicroFocus COBOL compiler, which you can read more about at www.microfocus.com) support extensions to the ACCEPT and DISPLAY commands to retrieve and return variables passed from a Web page.

The following example demonstrates how the ACCEPT statement retrieves Web page data:

```
01 INPUT-PAGE IS EXTERNAL-FORM.
   03 WS-NAME PIC X(30) IDENTIFIED BY "CNAME".
   03 WS-ADDR1 PIC X(30) IDENTIFIED BY "CADDR1".

   ACCEPT INPUT-PAGE.
```

The following DISPLAY statement returns Web page data:

```
01 ERROR-PAGE IS EXTERNAL-FORM IDENTIFIED BY "ERROR".
   03 ERROR-MSG1 PIC X(60) IDENTIFIED BY "E_MSG1".

MOVE "INVALID DETAILS ENTERED" TO ERROR-MSG1
DISPLAY ERROR-PAGE
```

Consult your specific compiler and Web server documentation for more information on using your COBOL applications as CGI applications.

Object-Oriented COBOL

Object-Oriented COBOL (OOCOBOL) enables facilities to develop object-oriented programs using the COBOL programming language. OOCOBOL provides the ability to:

+ Define classes, comprising class object definitions and object definitions

+ Define data encapsulated inside class objects and objects

+ Define methods for class objects and objects

+ Use inheritance and define subclasses

+ Use polymorphism and interfaces

+ Define data items able to hold references to objects

+ Call the methods defined by an object

+ Create and manage objects

+ Use objects as a normal part of COBOL programming in developing new programs and maintaining existing programs

An *object* is an entity that's made up of data and methods. All objects belong to a class. A class describes the structure of the data and the methods that apply to all the objects that are members of that class. A class also has a single class object with data and methods. The class object is an object that acts as a creator of objects.

Each object has an interface that's made up of the names and parameters for each method supported by the object. Each class defines two interfaces: an interface defining the methods supported by the class object (the class object interface), and the interface to be supported by each instance of the class.

Interfaces independent of class objects or class instances may be defined by listing the method names and parameter specifications supported by those interfaces. Interfaces can be specified in the declaration of an object identifier to restrict the objects that may be referred to by that identifier. Conformance is another name for a relationship between interfaces. An interface is said to conform to another interface if an object that implements all the methods specified in the first interface may be used any place in an object that implements all the methods specified in the second interface.

A request to execute a named method on a given object is called an *invocation*. Invocations may be specified in two ways. An in-line method invocation is indicated by two contiguous colons (::).

For example, the following invokes method `MY_METHOD` of object `OBJ`, with parameter `PARM`:

```
OBJ::MY_METHOD(PARM)
```

A method may be explicitly called using the `INVOKE` command.

An example of the `INVOKE` command would be as follows:

```
INVOKE OBJ "FOO" USING PARM RETURNING ANS
```

The `INVOKE` statement allows the name of the method to be invoked to be contained in a variable. In addition, parameters can be passed `BY CONTENT` (by value) or `BY REFERENCE`, and these options can be specified separately for each parameter in different `INVOKE` statements.

The procedural code in an object is placed in methods. Each method has its own method-name and its own `DATA DIVISION` and `PROCEDURE DIVISION`. When a method is invoked, the procedural code it contains is executed. A method is invoked by specifying a reference to the object and the name of the method. A method can take parameters and return data items. Data defined within a method can only be used within that method. Methods are an extension of program nesting (***see also*** Part I for more information about nesting).

The structure of a method definition is:

```
IDENTIFICATION DIVISION.
METHOD-ID.  method-name-1
       { PUBLIC } or
    IS { RESTRICTED } [PROTOTYPE]
       [OF [CLASS-OBJECT OF] class-name-1] or
       { PRIVATE }

[Method-Environment-Division]

[DATA DIVISION.
  Method-Data-Definitions]

[PROCEDURE DIVISION
    [ { INPUT } or
       USING {{ OUTPUT } data-name-1 } ...
            RETURNING data-name-2 or
       { I-O } ]
Method Procedure Statements]
END METHOD method-name-1.
```

The life cycle of an object begins when it is created and ends when it is destroyed. An object of a given class is created using a CBL-CREATE command associated with the class object for that class.

Object classes may be defined as any of the following:

✦ **Transient:** If a class is transient, the class objects and objects of the class are destroyed automatically when the program terminates.

✦ **Persistent:** If a class is persistent, the class object and objects of the class are destroyed only when a CBL-DISCARD method is invoked on them.

✦ **Collectable:** If a class is collectable, it lasts until the program terminates — just like transient objects — but collectable objects can be destroyed before the program terminates by the run unit's garbage collector, when they can no longer be referenced by transient objects within the run unit. (If a reference to a transient object is stored in the object data or class object data of a persistent object, the results of using this reference are undefined.)

Polymorphism is a feature that allows a given statement to do different things. In OOCOBOL, the ability for a data item to contain various objects of different classes means that a method using the same name on that data item can define using a number of different parameters and parameter types.

Sometimes, the correct method can be identified before the program is run, but generally the correct method is not determined until the program is running.

While object-oriented COBOL features are not currently part of the ANSI-85 standard, some compilers do support a subset of these features. In the next ANSI standard version of COBOL, ANSI-97, these features will officially become part of the programming language. Compilers that support OOCOBOL features today include:

✦ **Hitachi COBOL:** www.zoosoft.com/jp1/5a.html

✦ **IBM VisualAge for COBOL:** www.software.ibm.com/ad/cobol

✦ **MicroFocus COBOL:** www.microfocus.com

✦ **NiGSuN International:** www.nigsun.es

Using COBOL with CICS

IBM mainframes still continue to dominate the business information processing industry, and result in some of the more significant application considerations.

Many legacy COBOL applications written for IBM mainframes are closely interrelated with IBM CICS (Customer Information Control System). CICS is IBM's on-line transaction processing environment. CICS provides COBOL applications with the ability to create interactive user interfaces that handle very large transaction volumes with fast response times. CICS works closely with IBM's SNA (System Network Architecture) to provide application interface support on a wide variety of terminals.

SNA overview

In the early '70s, IBM discovered that enterprising customers required highly reliable and redundant communications networks to distribute mission-critical applications. In response, IBM developed Systems Network Architecture (SNA). SNA is designed to work well as long as communications equipment is properly installed and managed by a competent staff.

An SNA network is comprised of host systems (mainframes or AS/400s), terminals (or PC clients running terminal emulation software), printers, communication controllers, and cluster controllers. Terminals and printers connect to cluster controllers. Cluster controllers connect directly to the host or communications controller. The terminals, printers, communication controllers, and cluster controllers are generally referred to as nodes. Nodes are endpoints or linkages in the network.

Calling CICS from COBOL

CICS provides more than just an environment for building user interfaces, it also includes a dispatcher, storage control, task control, file control, and OLTP (on-line transaction processing). CICS abstracts many of these system-specific tasks from the application programmer.

While CICS began as an IBM mainframe-specific sub system, it is now supported on a number of different platforms, including: OS/2, AIX (IBM's version of UNIX), MVS/ESA (IBM's mainframe environment), AS/400, HP-UX, Digital OSF, Siemens SINIX, and Sun Solaris. CICS applications are supported for clients running DOS, OS/2, Windows, Macintosh, and UNIX.

The CICS interface is standardized across platforms, and is a fairly straightforward interface that can be directly embedded into your COBOL applications.

The following example illustrates a basic CICS routine:

```
EXEC CICS READ
     FILE(WS-FILE-NAME)
     INTO(WS-FILE-AREA)
     RIDFLD(WS-KEY-AREA)
     GTEQ
     RESP(WS-RESP)
END-EXEC
```

This COBOL example shows an attempt to READ a VSAM record INTO working storage for further processing. The COBOL READ statement (not to be confused with the CICS READ command) is not valid in CICS because it uses operating system (OS) services.

This is not permitted in CICS because all OS services are performed by CICS for integrity and availability reasons. The RIDFLD option is specifying the Record IDentifier FieLD or "key" to use. GTEQ is specifying GreaTer than or EQual to the RIDFLD. RESP indicates to place the RESPonse code in the WS-RESP field. Note that "EXEC CICS" is short for "EXECUTE CICS," and "END-EXEC" delimits the end of this particular COBOL CICS command.

The CICS command interface is common across multiple platforms. When a COBOL application is developed that uses CICS, a translator program is run which converts the EXEC CICS calls embedded in your application into COBOL CALL commands.

The following sample application code illustrates a very basic example; it displays system information and the last function key entered:

```
IDENTIFICATION DIVISION.
  PROGRAM-ID.    KEYMAP.

  ENVIRONMENT DIVISION.
  EJECT

  DATA DIVISION.

  WORKING-STORAGE SECTION.

      01  WS-CONSTANTS.
          05  WS-PROGRAM-ID          PIC X(8)
                                      VALUE 'KEYMAP'.
          05  WS-TRANS-ID            PIC X(4)
                                      VALUE 'NESA'.
          05  WS-MAP-NAME            PIC X(8)
                                      VALUE 'DCNESAM '.
          05  WS-MAPSET-NAME         PIC X(08)
                                      VALUE 'DCNESAS '.
```

(continued)

(continued)

```
        05  WS-COMMAREA-LENGTH        PIC S9(04)
                                      COMP VALUE +8 .
        05  WS-MESSAGE-LENGTH         PIC S9(04)
                                      COMP VALUE +79.
        05  WS-ERRMSG                 PIC X(40)
          VALUE 'NESA TRANSACTION TERMINATED DUE TO ERROR'.
        05  WS-ENDMSG                 PIC X(22)
          VALUE 'NESA TRANSACTION ENDED'.
    01  WS-COMMAREA.
        05  WS-CA-PGMID               PIC X(08)
                                      VALUE SPACES.
    01  WS-SWITCHES.
        05  WS-FIRST-TIME-SW          PIC X(01)  VALUE 'Y'.
            88  FIRST-TIME                       VALUE 'Y'.
            88  NOT-FIRST-TIME                   VALUE 'N'.
        05  WS-RETURN-TO-TRAN-SW      PIC X(01)  VALUE 'Y'.
            88  RETURN-TO-TRAN                   VALUE 'Y'.
            88  END-TRAN                         VALUE 'N'.
    01  WS-HOLD-AREAS.
        05  WS-MESSAGE                PIC X(79)
                                      VALUE SPACES.
        05  WS-ABSTIME                PIC S9(16) COMP.
        05  WS-SYSDATE                PIC X(08)
                                      VALUE SPACES.
        05  WS-SYSTIME                PIC X(08)
                                      VALUE SPACES.
        05  WS-EIBDATE                PIC 9(05) VALUE ZERO.
        05  WS-RESP                   PIC S9(08) COMP
                                      VALUE ZERO.
    EJECT
    COPY DFHAID.
    EJECT
    COPY DCNESASD.
    EJECT
    LINKAGE SECTION.

        01  DFH-COMM-AREA             PIC X(08).
        EJECT

PROCEDURE DIVISION.
    0000-PROGRAM-DCNESAMP.
        PERFORM 1000-INIT.
        IF NOT-FIRST-TIME
            PERFORM 2000-GET-MAP.
        PERFORM 3000-SEND-MAP.
        IF RETURN-TO-TRAN
            PERFORM 8000-RETURN
        ELSE
            PERFORM 9000-END-TRANSACTION.
        GOBACK.

    1000-INIT.
        EXEC CICS HANDLE CONDITION
            ERROR(9200-HANDLE-ERROR)
        END-EXEC.
```

```
              IF EIBCALEN = 0
                  MOVE LOW-VALUES TO DCNESAMO
                  MOVE WS-PROGRAM-ID TO WS-CA-PGMID
              ELSE
              IF EIBCALEN = WS-COMMAREA-LENGTH
                  MOVE 'N' TO WS-FIRST-TIME-SW
                  MOVE DFH-COMM-AREA TO WS-COMMAREA
              ELSE
                  PERFORM 9200-HANDLE-ERROR.
          EJECT
          2000-GET-MAP.
              MOVE LOW-VALUES TO DCNESAMI.
              EXEC CICS RECEIVE MAP(WS-MAP-NAME)
                                MAPSET(WS-MAPSET-NAME)
                                INTO(DCNESAMI)
                            RESP(WS-RESP)
              END-EXEC.
              IF ENDI = 'END' OR 'end'
                  MOVE 'N' TO WS-RETURN-TO-TRAN-SW.
          3000-SEND-MAP.
              PERFORM 3100-PROCESS-EIBAID.
              EXEC CICS ASKTIME
                        ABSTIME(WS-ABSTIME)
                        RESP(WS-RESP)
              END-EXEC.
              EXEC CICS FORMATTIME
                        ABSTIME(WS-ABSTIME)
                        MMDDYY(WS-SYSDATE)
                        DATESEP('/')
                        TIME(WS-SYSTIME)
                        TIMESEP(':')
                        RESP(WS-RESP)
              END-EXEC.
              MOVE WS-SYSDATE TO DATEO.
              MOVE WS-SYSTIME TO TIMEO.
              MOVE EIBDATE TO WS-EIBDATE.
              MOVE WS-EIBDATE TO DATEJO.
              MOVE EIBTRMID TO TERMIDO.
              IF FIRST-TIME OR EIBAID = DFHCLEAR OR DFHCLRP
                  EXEC CICS SEND MAP(WS-MAP-NAME)
                                 MAPSET(WS-MAPSET-NAME)
                                 FROM(DCNESAMO)
                            ERASE FREEKB
                  END-EXEC
              ELSE
                  EXEC CICS SEND MAP(WS-MAP-NAME)
                                 MAPSET(WS-MAPSET-NAME)
                                 FROM(DCNESAMO)
                            ERASEAUP FREEKB DATAONLY
                  END-EXEC.
          EJECT

          3100-PROCESS-EIBAID.
              IF EIBAID = DFHNULL MOVE 'NULL ' TO KEYO
              ELSE IF EIBAID = DFHENTER MOVE 'ENTER' TO KEYO
              ELSE IF EIBAID = DFHCLEAR MOVE 'CLEAR' TO KEYO
```

(continued)

(continued)

```
                        ELSE IF EIBAID = DFHCLRP  MOVE 'CLRP ' TO KEYO
                        ELSE IF EIBAID = DFHPEN   MOVE 'PEN  ' TO KEYO
                        ELSE IF EIBAID = DFHOPID  MOVE 'OPID ' TO KEYO
                        ELSE IF EIBAID = DFHMSRE  MOVE 'MSRE ' TO KEYO
                        ELSE IF EIBAID = DFHSTRF  MOVE 'STRF ' TO KEYO
                        ELSE IF EIBAID = DFHTRIG  MOVE 'TRIG ' TO KEYO
                        ELSE IF EIBAID = DFHPA1   MOVE 'PA1  ' TO KEYO
                        ELSE IF EIBAID = DFHPA2   MOVE 'PA2  ' TO KEYO
                        ELSE IF EIBAID = DFHPA3   MOVE 'PA3  ' TO KEYO
                        ELSE IF EIBAID = DFHPF1   MOVE 'PF1  ' TO KEYO
                        ELSE IF EIBAID = DFHPF2   MOVE 'PF2  ' TO KEYO
                        ELSE IF EIBAID = DFHPF3   MOVE 'PF3  ' TO KEYO
                        ELSE IF EIBAID = DFHPF4   MOVE 'PF4  ' TO KEYO
                        ELSE IF EIBAID = DFHPF5   MOVE 'PF5  ' TO KEYO
                        ELSE IF EIBAID = DFHPF6   MOVE 'PF6  ' TO KEYO
                        ELSE IF EIBAID = DFHPF7   MOVE 'PF7  ' TO KEYO
                        ELSE IF EIBAID = DFHPF8   MOVE 'PF8  ' TO KEYO
                        ELSE IF EIBAID = DFHPF9   MOVE 'PF9  ' TO KEYO
                        ELSE IF EIBAID = DFHPF10  MOVE 'PF10 ' TO KEYO
                        ELSE IF EIBAID = DFHPF11  MOVE 'PF11 ' TO KEYO
                        ELSE IF EIBAID = DFHPF12  MOVE 'PF12 ' TO KEYO
                        ELSE IF EIBAID = DFHPF13  MOVE 'PF13 ' TO KEYO
                        ELSE IF EIBAID = DFHPF14  MOVE 'PF14 ' TO KEYO
                        ELSE IF EIBAID = DFHPF15  MOVE 'PF15 ' TO KEYO
                        ELSE IF EIBAID = DFHPF16  MOVE 'PF16 ' TO KEYO
                        ELSE IF EIBAID = DFHPF17  MOVE 'PF17 ' TO KEYO
                        ELSE IF EIBAID = DFHPF18  MOVE 'PF18 ' TO KEYO
                        ELSE IF EIBAID = DFHPF19  MOVE 'PF19 ' TO KEYO
                        ELSE IF EIBAID = DFHPF20  MOVE 'PF20 ' TO KEYO
                        ELSE IF EIBAID = DFHPF21  MOVE 'PF21 ' TO KEYO
                        ELSE IF EIBAID = DFHPF22  MOVE 'PF22 ' TO KEYO
                        ELSE IF EIBAID = DFHPF23  MOVE 'PF23 ' TO KEYO
                        ELSE IF EIBAID = DFHPF24  MOVE 'PF24 ' TO KEYO
                        ELSE MOVE '?????' TO KEYO.
                EJECT
                8000-RETURN.
                    EXEC CICS RETURN
                                TRANSID(WS-TRANS-ID)
                                COMMAREA(WS-COMMAREA)
                                LENGTH(WS-COMMAREA-LENGTH)
                        END-EXEC.

                9000-END-TRANSACTION.
                    MOVE WS-ENDMSG TO WS-MESSAGE.
                    PERFORM 9900-TERMINATE.

                9200-HANDLE-ERROR.
                    MOVE WS-ERRMSG TO WS-MESSAGE.
                    PERFORM 9900-TERMINATE.

                9900-TERMINATE.
                    EXEC CICS SEND
                                FROM(WS-MESSAGE)
                                LENGTH(WS-MESSAGE-LENGTH)
                                ERASE
```

```
END-EXEC.
EXEC CICS SEND CONTROL
          FREEKB
END-EXEC.
EXEC CICS RETURN
END-EXEC.
```

Surfing for CICS Web sites

It's not possible to cover the CICS application programming interface in detail here. More information on CICS is provided at the following Web sites:

- ✦ **The Official IBM CICS Web Site:** www.hursley.ibm.com/cics

- ✦ **CICS Reference Manuals On-Line:** ppdbooks.pok.ibm.com/cgi-bin/bookmgr/bookmgr.cmd/Shelves?filter=CICS

- ✦ **MVSHelp:** www.mvshelp.com

Part XI

Solving the Year-2000 Problem

Tick-tock, tick-tock, tick-tock. Do you hear it? It's the countdown to the new millennium. Are you and your applications ready for the year 2000? Do you under-stand the challenge and the impact on your business? And how do you begin and manage your year-2000 upgrades?

It's really not that hard to understand and begin working on the problem. The keys are to start as soon as possible and to develop a methodical strategy of implementation and testing.

Remember, every day that you wait, the clock ticks closer to the year 2000, and if your program uses future dates, the year-2000 phenomenon can affect programs even earlier than that! It's important to get started with your year-2000 development efforts as soon as possible. It's not as daunting a task as you may think — this part takes you through a step-by-step process that can help to get your projects on the move.

In this part . . .

✔ **Understanding year-2000 issues and how they affect your applications**

✔ **Attacking the year-2000 problem with a step-by-step guide**

✔ **Building a year-2000 development team and creating a project scope**

✔ **Managing your year-2000 development process**

✔ **Surfing the Web for more information about the year 2000 and application development**

Addressing the Issues

What's the big deal? Your programs have worked without a hitch since they were implemented. Why would they stop working when the year 2000 rolls around?

The biggest problem is the computer's use of only the last two digits to represent a year — instead of also storing the first two digits to represent the century. This strategy works well and is rather efficient as long as you remain in the 20th century. As soon as the year 2000 hits, things can really get fouled up. For example, years following the year 2000, which the computer sees as 01, 02, and so on, are interpreted to be numerically smaller than 97, 98, and 99. Throw in some addition and subtraction with those numbers, and things get even more messed up.

What's even more dangerous is that some programs interpret the dates 00 and 99 as special codes! As a result, the year-2000 problem could start creeping in during 1999!

The following table lists some of the common year-2000 date miscalculations that can occur along with examples of each kind of miscalculation:

Miscalculation Type	*Example*
Wrong century	A value of 01 is assumed to be 1901 instead of 2001.
Incorrect date arithmetic	Subtracting date values can lead to incorrect results: $2000 - 1966 = 34$, but $00 - 66 = -66$. Ouch!
Incorrect comparisons	When comparing dates, the future seems like the past (for example, $2000 > 1997$, but $00 < 97$).
Data integrity	Centuries simply get lost. The years 1895, 1995, and 2095 are all stored as just 95.
Reserved date value conflicts	Some programs interpret dates that contain the year 00 as invalid and keep 99 forever.
Incorrect leap-year calculation	2000 is a leap year.

Planning Your Project

So, you're ready to start tackling this year-2000 problem in your applications. It's about time!

Bringing a team together

One of the first and most important steps that you can take is to develop a year-2000 team. This team should have representation from all sectors of your company and should minimally include the following individuals:

+ A project leader, who will be responsible for carrying out and coordinating all analysis, development, testing, and integration.

+ Critical application users, whose feedback is essential in planning and understanding the applications that are currently deployed. These users bring a working knowledge of the critical applications, and they can help you to prioritize your development efforts.

+ A representative from the management team, who should help coordinate information and status reports with the rest of the management team.

+ A group of programmers, whose sole task is to solve the year-2000 problem. It's best if your programmers can concentrate their efforts on a single project.

The year-2000 project team should have complete control over its personnel and resources. You don't need Fred from Accounting pulling your lead programmer off a project to fix a minor problem. This is a project with a tight timeline and a fixed due date. You can't delay January 1, 2000 — and you need to be ready.

Defining your year-2000 goals

Any project or organization needs clear goals to be successful. I'm sure that you can think of companies that you've worked for that seemed to have ill-defined goals — I can certainly think of a few.

Without a goal, everyone goes off doing his or her own thing — which inevitably dooms a project. I suggest starting with a simple goal and definition. For example, your year-2000 team goal should be to update existing applications and resources so that they are "year-2000-ready."

I suggest defining a year-2000-ready application as one that, when used in the normal course of business, can correctly process, receive, provide, and report on all date data throughout the 20th and 21st centuries. Make this your team mantra.

Understanding the project scope

Don't be fooled — this is probably the most complex and far-reaching project that your company has ever taken on. It's not an isolated problem; it affects all levels of your business and the applications that the business relies on.

It takes a concerted effort to solve this problem on time. It's also one of the few projects that you encounter that truly has a fixed deadline — January 1, 2000. While "Year 2000" is a big project, it is quite doable and manageable. The keys are to stay focused, stay on time, and be methodical.

Updating Your Programs for the Year 2000

Getting your programs ready for the year 2000 requires a systematic approach. If you follow the advice in this section, you'll be ready when the calendar turns to January 1, 2000.

Step 1: Preparing your hardware and system software

If you're unsure whether your hardware and system software are year-2000-compliant, contact the appropriate vendors. It's important to do this before you begin updating your custom internal applications.

If your hardware and system software are relatively new (less than a few years), you're probably safe. You should check the documentation included with your system software to determine how dates are handled. If you use any special hardware devices, such as scanners, that also capture date information, you may need to check how these devices handle dates.

After you get your hardware and system software up to muster, the real fun begins — updating your internal applications.

Step 2: Assessing inventory and budgeting

This step may consume 5 to 10 percent of your project timeline. You need to roll up your sleeves and develop a complete inventory of your applications and data sources that are affected by the year-2000 issue.

An application is considered year-2000-compatible if it can process any and all dates in the 20th century (1900-1999) and the 21st century (2000-2099) without a problem.

Ideally, your organization has already compiled a list of all the applications that are in use and how they function. In the real world, this is often not the case. This is a divide-and-conquer problem for your year-2000 development team.

 If possible, have each department report which applications they are currently using. Although tools are available to help you with the process (such as software inventory and source code analysis tools), tapping the knowledge of a few key personnel may be more effective than using these tools.

Try to be as detailed as possible. This may take some snooping, because some applications may run in the background or run infrequently — these applications can be easily overlooked.

 Don't look at this inventory as a static document — undoubtedly something will be overlooked — but try to be as comprehensive as possible at the start of the project. This list becomes the basis for planning and budgeting.

After you create your detailed list, prioritize your applications and data sources. In this way, you can solve the most urgent needs first.

 At this stage, it's easy to panic — everything begins to look urgent and critical. Take a deep breath, and then take the time to make the appropriate assessments.

After you prioritize your list, develop some preliminary time and cost budgets to present to upper management. It's important that your CIO (Chief Information Officer) or other high-level information services personnel are involved as early as possible in your developmental efforts.

 When approaching management to secure funding for your development efforts, remember to keep the discussion on business issues. Don't get wrapped up in technical items. You are presenting a bottom-line issue. Show how and why these applications affect day-to-day operations.

Be prepared for a certain amount of compromise when developing your budget. Try to make it an incremental process that will be refined as you work your way through the project. The next step — code and data analysis — can help you assemble a firmer budget.

Step 3: Analyzing code, data, and resources

Code and data analysis is the first major step in your development effort. You can't get around it — you must crack open these applications, take a close look at their guts, and determine how they work.

You're looking for all the places in your application and its associated data where dates are used. You need to make sure that every place a date is used, the data and applications can now handle dates with centuries. Be sure to check all the nooks and crannies to make sure that you've found every place a date is used. Expect to consume 20 to 25 percent of your project timeline in this phase.

Hopefully, you can find supporting documentation for these applications — at a user and system level — that can help make the process easier. However, in many cases, the original developers have moved on or can't remember many of the programming details. As a result, you must take the time to understand each application and determine what other applications and data sources it affects. This is when you really begin to see what you're up against.

If you have quite a few applications that require modification, you may want to take a survey approach: Select a few applications to develop a basis for planning your timeline and resource requirements. While this may not always produce accurate results, it can give you a feel for what you're going to need.

Then comes the next big question: Do you have enough internal manpower and time to complete the projects on time? If not, consider outsourcing some part of the development effort. Remember, though, outsourcing adds another level of management to the process.

Step 4: Investigating your options

After you have a detailed understanding of your current applications, you need to figure out how you're going to fix the problem. Three main approaches can be used to handle date data:

+ **Expand year fields to hold century information.** This is the ideal approach to solving the year-2000 problem. Instead of carrying around two-digit dates, you now add the century and have four-digit dates.

   This is the best approach for applications that you think may be around for a while. However, it does require changes to your data and all applications that use your data. The approach may require the greatest level of short-term effort, but it pays off in long-term benefits.

+ **Infer the correct century.** With this approach, you create a century window, which is a 100-year interval where you assume that all two-digit dates can be found. For example, if your century window range is January 1, 1920, through December 21, 2019, you can assume that all two-digit dates that are greater than or equal to 20 are in the 1900s and all two-digit dates that are less than or equal to 19 are in the 2000s. You can make the century window a fixed interval or make the upper bound move with the current system date.

This approach works best for applications with a short-term life expectancy or as a short-term fix for strategic applications where you just don't have the full-blown fix.

Before you consider implementing this approach, you should determine if your application needs to process dates that are more than 100 years apart. If this is the case, then this approach doesn't work. The approach may also result in a loss of performance due to the extra logic that's required to determine the correct century. Make sure that you take performance issues into account during testing if you decide to implement this approach.

✦ **Compress the date to fit into two digits.** This is probably the least desirable approach. With this method, you convert four-digit years into another representation that can be stored in two bytes — such as a binary number or an unsigned packed decimal.

The drawbacks to this approach include the extra logic that's needed to convert the compressed-year data into a viewable form and the inability to quickly view and understand dates directly from your data source. Furthermore, you must still change both your programs and your data. Again, it's an approach for short-term, short-life-expectancy projects.

The number of interactions between programs and data may be quite large. It's not possible to fix all your problems overnight. You should tackle the year-2000 problem one application at a time. This may require you to develop bridge programs which convert data from the year-2000-compliant four-digit century to the older two-digit century used by applications which haven't been converted yet. These bridge programs allow you to phase in your year-2000 development.

Step 5: Modifying code and data

After you perform a detailed analysis of your applications and select an approach to fixing the date problem, the dig-in-and-get-it-done work begins. Typically this consumes 20 to 25 percent of your project timeline.

Before you modify any program or data, make sure that you have a backup copy for archival purposes. Never try to work on live applications or data — make sure that you have a separate area for development and testing. The last thing you want to do is to start mucking around with the current production copies of applications — unless you want to get fired fast!

A number of tasks are involved in this phase, including the following:

✦ Modifying the libraries that are used by your applications

✦ Modifying data sources as necessary

✦ Modifying the source code, screens, reports, and forms

✦ Implementing your chosen date-representation methodology

You won't find a magic wand here. While applications are available that purport to automate the conversion process, research and my own experience suggest that, at best, these applications save you 10 to 20 percent of the time required.

Sometimes it's just easier to go through the code step by step and make the necessary changes by hand. Tools aren't going to find all the potential problem areas and the subtle nuances of your applications.

Before a programmer is allowed to crack the seal of an application, he or she should be fairly competent in the goals of the program, understand the date approach chosen, and, if possible, have a designated contact within the organization that relies on the applications to answer any questions.

I can't stress this enough: The most important facet of the process is to stay focused. Resist the temptation to make other changes if possible. Take it step by step and line by line, and work your way through the program.

Step 6: Testing and integration

The most critical phase of any project is testing. Don't underestimate the importance or the time requirements of this phase. Typically, this portion consumes 40 to 45 percent of your project timeline.

Expect to take about twice as much time as you spent on the implementation phase to thoroughly test and integrate your application.

A number of tasks are involved in the testing and implementation phase, including the following:

✦ Developing a detailed test plan

✦ Performing integration and systems tests

+ Integrating changes to any library or shared resources

+ Performing acceptance testing

+ Moving the application into the production environment

The focus of your testing should be on your mission-critical applications. Don't waste a lot of time testing applications that pose little risk.

Developing a test plan is a detailed and time-consuming process. The advantage, though, is that developing a plan to test your application can begin and continue in parallel with the process of updating your applications for year-2000-compliance. This process may return some input, but these tasks can proceed independently.

It's important to create a separate, isolated environment for your testing. Make sure that you're not relying on any resource that won't be available in the production environment — such as faster or newer hardware or systems software — especially if you're conducting performance testing.

When you begin to integrate changes to libraries or shared resources, you need to rerun your tests on other applications that may also be affected. A number of tools are available to help you automate the testing process. Software testing tools automate the testing process through:

+ Generating test input data

+ Automating test runs

+ Evaluating program output after a test run

+ Logging and comparing previous results

+ The ability to test your applications in a consistent manner as many times as required

Testing tools can help you ensure the keys to good application testing — consistency and completeness. The following companies provide software testing tools:

+ **Aonix:** 595 Market Street, 10th Floor, San Francisco, CA, 94105. Phone: 415-543-0900. Web site: www.aonix.com

+ **CenterLine Software:** 10 Fawcett Street, Cambridge, MA, 02138. Phone: 617-498-3000. Web site: www.centerline.com/home.html

+ **Compuware:** 31440 Northwestern Highway, Farmington Hills, MI, 48334-2564. Phone: 800-521-9353. Web site: www.compuware.com

+ **Mercury Interactive:** 470 Potrero Avenue, Sunnyvale, CA, 94086. Phone: 408-523-9900. Web site: www.merc-int.com

+ **Rational Software:** 18880 Homestead Road, Cupertino, CA, 95014. Phone: 800-728-1212. Web site: www.rational.com

+ **VisionSoft:** Pruneyard Towers, 1999 South Bascom Avenue, Suite 700, Campbell, CA, 95008-9872. Phone: 408-879-2672. Web site: www.vsonline.com

Testing tools can automatically run the same test suites repeatedly. (A *test suite* is a set of input data or program commands that test how a program operates.)

These tools can give you a sense of security, but don't forget to implement real-world performance testing as well. Real-world testing involves testing your applications with a set of input data or commands that would be commonly used for day-to-day processing.

To implement real-world testing, allow a small number of users to run and interact with your program before you move it over into production. If possible, try to run mission-critical applications in parallel before you implement a complete cut-over.

Step 7: Popping open the bubbly

If all goes well, you end up with updated applications that are ready for the year 2000 and beyond! You won't find any rocket science or magic about the project. Implementing a successful year-2000 conversion is all about good planning and project management. If you and your company already apply good project management techniques, you shouldn't have any problems.

Year-2000 Resources on the Internet

The Internet is full of year-2000 Web sites, where you can get the latest information and additional resources for planning and implementing your year-2000 projects. Check out some of the following sites for more information:

+ **2K Times:** www.bluemarble.net/~storageu/y2k.htm

+ **Bill Cook's Y2K Resource Links:** pw1.netcom.com/~wjcook/resource.html

+ **Cinderella Web Site:** www.cinderella.co.za/

+ **Com.Links Magazine:** www.comlinks.com/

+ **Dr. Kappelman:** www-lan.unt.edu/cobabak/www/bcis/faculty/kappelma/

- ✦ **Goal 2000 Web Page:** www.ourworld.compuserve.com/homepages/Goal2000/

- ✦ **Information Technology Association of America (ITAA):** www.itaa.org/

- ✦ **IT Policy OnRamp:** www.itpolicy.gsa.gov/

- ✦ **Jerry S. Odum's Year 2000 Info Page:** www.jsodum.com/y2kmenu.html

- ✦ **Larry Towner's Year 2000 Bibliography:** www.ttuhsc.edu/pages/year2000/y2k_bib.htm

- ✦ **Legal and Management Information on Year 2000:** www.y2k.com/

- ✦ **MITRE Year 2000 for the Electronic Systems Center:** www.mitre.org/research/y2k/

- ✦ **New Millennium: The Year 2000 Problem — People, Programs And Organizations:** mach10.utica.kaman.com/cgi-bin/key1?13:31

- ✦ **PA News Centre:** www.pa.press.net/tech/

- ✦ **Pirkle and Associates:** www.pirkle-websites.com/

- ✦ **Rx 2000 Solutions Institute:** www.rx2000.org/

- ✦ **STSC Reengineering Group:** stsc.hill.af.mil/RENG/index.html#2000

- ✦ **The National Bulletin Board For Year 2000:** www.it2000.com/

- ✦ **The Year 2000 Information Center:** www.year2000.com/cgi-bin/y2k/year2000.cgi

- ✦ **The Year 2000 Problem:** www.year2000.co.uk/

- ✦ **Thelen, Marrin, Johnson & Bridges LLP:** www.tmjb.com/practice/practice.cfm?ID=y2k

- ✦ **Unisys:** www.unisys.com/marketplace/year2000/index.html

- ✦ **Westergaard Year 2000:** www.y2ktimebomb.com

- ✦ **Y2K Links:** www.y2klinks.com/

- ✦ **Yahoo's Year 2000 Page:** www.yahoo.com/Business_and_Economy/Companies/Computers/Software/Systems_and_Utilities/Year_2000_Problem/

- ✦ **Year 2000 Date Problem Support Center:** www.compinfo.co.uk/y2k.htm

- ✦ **Year 2000 Information Network:** web.idirect.com/~mbsprog

In addition, the book *Year 2000 Solutions For Dummies,* by K.C. Bourne, published by IDG Books Worldwide, Inc., provides a detailed look at the year-2000 question.

Part XII

COBOL Formats

This part provides a formal definition of the entire COBOL programming language. I break down each area of a COBOL program. The format of each division and all of the COBOL verbs are provided here for your reference. Use this part if you need to quickly determine the syntax of any COBOL division.

In this part . . .

✓ Using the IDENTIFICATION DIVISION

✓ Caring for the environment with the ENVIRONMENT DIVISION

✓ Defining files and the records they contain with the DATA DIVISION

✓ Creating the working section of your program with the PROCEDURE DIVISION

✓ Making your COBOL application go using command verbs

IDENTIFICATION DIVISION

The following code presents the syntax of the IDENTIFICATION DIVISION (***see also*** Part II for more information about the IDENTIFICATION DIVISION):

```
IDENTIFICATION DIVISION.

PROGRAM-ID. program-name-1
     [IS {[RECURSIVE or
          COMMON or
          INITIAL]} PROGRAM].

[AUTHOR. [comment-entry-1]...]

[INSTALLATION. [comment-entry-2]...]

[DATE-WRITTEN. [comment-entry-3]...]

[DATE-COMPILED. [comment-entry-4]...]

[SECURITY. [comment-entry-5]...]
```

ENVIRONMENT DIVISION

The following code presents the syntax of the ENVIRONMENT DIVISION (***see also*** Part III for more information about the ENVIRONMENT DIVISION):

```
[ENVIRONMENT DIVISION.

  [CONFIGURATION SECTION.

    [SOURCE-COMPUTER. [computer-name-1
         [WITH DEBUGGING MODE].]]

    [OBJECT-COMPUTER. [computer-name-2
      [MEMORY SIZE integer-1
       {WORDS or CHARACTERS or MODULES}]
    [PROGRAM COLLATING SEQUENCE IS alphabet-name-1]
    [SEGMENT-LIMIT IS segment-number].]]

    [SPECIAL-NAMES. [[implementor-name-1
      {IS mnemonic-name-1
       [ON STATUS IS condition-name-1
    [OFF STATUS IS condition-name-2]] or
  IS mnemonic-name-2
    [OFF STATUS IS condition-name-2
    [ON STATUS IS condition-name-1]] or
  ON STATUS IS condition-name-1
    [OFF STATUS IS condition-name-2] or
  OFF STATUS IS condition-name-2
    [ON STATUS IS condition-name-1]}]...
```

```
                 [ALPHABET alphabet-name-1 IS
                   {STANDARD-1 or
                   STANDARD-2 or
                   NATIVE or
        EBCDIC or
                   implementor-name-2 or
                   {literal-1
                     [{THROUGH or THRU} literal-2 or
                     {ALSO literal-3}...]}...}]...
                 [SYMBOLIC CHARACTERS {symbolic-character-1}...
                   {IS or ARE} {integer-1}...}...
                   [IN alphabet-name-2]]...
                 [CLASS class-name-1 IS {literal-4
                   [{THROUGH or THRU} literal-5]}...]...
            [CURRENCY SIGN IS literal-6]
              [DECIMAL POINT IS COMMA].]]]

              [INPUT-OUTPUT SECTION.
              FILE-CONTROL.
            {file-control-entry}...

              [I-O-CONTROL.
                [[RERUN [ON {file-name-1 or
                                implementor-name-1}] EVERY}
                   {{END OF {REEL or UNIT} or
                     integer-1 RECORDS} OF file-name-2 or
                     integer-2 CLOCK-UNITS or
                     condition-name-1}]...
                 [SAME
                   [RECORD or
                    SORT or
                    SORT-MERGE] AREA FOR file-name-3
                                     {file-name-4}...]...
                 [MULTIPLE FILE TAPE CONTAINS
                   {file-name-5 [POSITION integer-3]}...]....]]]]
```

FILE CONTROL ENTRY

The FILE CONTROL ENTRY SECTION associates a program name with an external file (***see also*** Part III for more information):

SEQUENTIAL FILE:

```
SELECT [OPTIONAL] file-name-1
     ASSIGN {TO {implementor-name-1 or literal-1}...}or
        {USING  data-name-9}
     [RESERVE integer-1 [AREA or AREAS]]
     [[ORGANIZATION IS] SEQUENTIAL]
     [PADDING CHARACTER IS {data-name-1 or literal-2}]
        [RECORD DELIMITER IS
           {STANDARD-1 or implementor-name-2}]
     [ACCESS MODE IS SEQUENTIAL]
     [FILE STATUS IS data-name-2].
```

(continued)

(continued)

```
RELATIVE FILE:

SELECT [OPTIONAL] file-name-1
    ASSIGN {TO {implementor-name-1 or literal-1}...}or
        {USING  data-name-9}
    [RESERVE integer-1 [AREA or AREAS]]
    [[ORGANIZATION IS] [RELATIVE]
        [ACCESS MODE IS
            {SEQUENTIAL [RELATIVE KEY IS data-name-1] or
            {RANDOM or
             DYNAMIC}
             RELATIVE KEY IS data-name-1}]
    [FILE STATUS IS data-name-2].

INDEXED FILE:

SELECT [OPTIONAL] file-name-1
    ASSIGN {TO {implementor-name-1 or literal-1}...}or
        {USING  data-name-9}
    [RESERVE integer-1 [AREA or AREAS]]
    [[ORGANIZATION IS] INDEXED
    [ACCESS MODE IS
        {SEQUENTIAL or RANDOM or DYNAMIC}]
    RECORD KEY IS data-name-1
        [ALTERNATE RECORD KEY IS data-name-2
        [WITH DUPLICATES]]...
    [FILE STATUS IS data-name-3].

SORT OR MERGE FILE:

  SELECT file-name-1 ASSIGN TO
{implementor-name-1 or literal-1}....

REPORT FILE:

SELECT [OPTIONAL] file-name-1
    ASSIGN TO{implementor-name-1 or literal-1}...
    [RESERVE integer-1 [AREA or AREAS]]
    [[ORGANIZATION IS] SEQUENTIAL]
    [PADDING CHARACTER IS {data-name-1 or literal-2}]
        [RECORD DELIMITER IS
            {STANDARD-1 or implementor-name-2}]
    [ACCESS MODE IS SEQUENTIAL]
    [FILE STATUS IS data-name-2].
```

DATA DIVISION

The following code presents the syntax for the DATA DIVISION (*see also* Part IV for more information on the DATA DIVISION):

```
[DATA DIVISION.
```

```
[FILE SECTION.
```

```
[file-description-entry
    {record-description-entry}... or
sort-merge-file-description-entry
    {record-description-entry}... or
report-file-description-entry]...]
```

[WORKING-STORAGE SECTION.

```
    [77-level-description-entry or
        record-description-entry]...]
```

[LINKAGE SECTION.

```
    [77-level-description-entry or
        record-description-entry]...]
```

[COMMUNICATION SECTION.

```
    [communication-description-entry
        [record-description-entry]...]...]
```

[REPORT SECTION.

```
    [report-description-entry
        {report-group-description-entry}...]...]]
```

FILE DESCRIPTION ENTRY

The FILE DESCRIPTION ENTRY SECTION describes the record structure of the files used by your program (***see also*** Part IV for more information):

SEQUENTIAL FILE:

FD *file-name-1*

    [IS **EXTERNAL**]

    [IS **GLOBAL**]

       [**BLOCK** CONTAINS
        [*integer-1* **TO**] *integer-2*
  {**RECORDS** *or* **CHARACTERS**}]

       [**RECORD**
        {CONTAINS *integer-3* CHARACTERS *or*
        IS **VARYING** IN SIZE [[FROM *integer-4*]
        [**TO** *integer-5*] CHARACTERS] *or*
        [**DEPENDING** ON *data-name-1*] *or*
        CONTAINS *integer-6* **TO** *integer-7* CHARACTERS}]

       [**LABEL** {**RECORD** IS *or* **RECORDS** ARE}
  {**STANDARD** *or* **OMITTED**}]

(continued)

(continued)

```
            [VALUE OF {implementor-name-1 IS
                {data-name-2 or literal-1}}...]

        [DATA {RECORD IS or RECORDS ARE}{data-name-3}...]

            [LINAGE IS {data-name-4 or integer-8}
                LINES [WITH FOOTING AT
                        {data-name-5 or integer-9}]

                [LINES AT TOP
                        {data-name-6 or integer-10}]
                [LINES AT BOTTOM {data-name-7 or integer-11}]]

        [CODE SET IS alphabet-name-1].
```

RELATIVE FILE:

```
            FD file-name-1
                [IS EXTERNAL]

        [IS GLOBAL]

            [BLOCK CONTAINS
                [integer-1 TO] integer-2
        {RECORDS or CHARACTERS}]

            [RECORD
                {CONTAINS integer-3 CHARACTERS or
                 IS VARYING IN SIZE [[FROM integer-4]
                    [TO integer-5] CHARACTERS] or
                 [DEPENDING ON data-name-1] or
                 CONTAINS integer-6 TO integer-7 CHARACTERS}]

            [LABEL {RECORD IS or RECORDS ARE}
                {STANDARD or OMITTED}]

            [VALUE OF {implementor-name-1 IS
                {data-name-2 or literal-1}}...]

        [DATA {RECORD IS or RECORDS ARE}
                {data-name-3}...].
```

INDEXED FILE:

```
            FD file-name-1
                [IS EXTERNAL]

        [IS GLOBAL]

            [BLOCK CONTAINS
                [integer-1 TO] integer-2
        {RECORDS or CHARACTERS}]

            [RECORD
                {CONTAINS integer-3 CHARACTERS or
                 IS VARYING IN SIZE [[FROM integer-4]
```

```
            [TO integer-5] CHARACTERS] or
            [DEPENDING ON data-name-1] or
            CONTAINS integer-6 TO integer-7 CHARACTERS}]

       [LABEL {RECORD IS or RECORDS ARE}
            {STANDARD or OMITTED}]

       [VALUE OF {implementor-name-1 IS
            {data-name-2 or literal-1}}...]

    [DATA {RECORD IS or RECORDS ARE}
            {data-name-3}...].

SORT-MERGE FILE:

  SD file-name-1

       [RECORD
            {CONTAINS integer-3 CHARACTERS or
            IS VARYING IN SIZE [[FROM integer-4]
            [TO integer-5] CHARACTERS] or
            [DEPENDING ON data-name-1] or
            CONTAINS integer-6 TO integer-7 CHARACTERS}]

       [DATA {RECORD IS or RECORDS ARE}
            {data-name-3}...].

       [BLOCK CONTAINS
            [integer-1 TO] integer-2
     {RECORDS or CHARACTERS}]

       [LABEL {RECORD IS or RECORDS ARE}
     {STANDARD or OMITTED}]

       [VALUE OF {implementor-name-1 IS
            {data-name-2 or literal-1}}...]

    [LINAGE IS {data-name-4 or integer-8}

          LINES [WITH FOOTING AT
                    {data-name-5 or integer-9}]

          [LINES AT TOP
                    {data-name-6 or integer-10}]
          [LINES AT BOTTOM {data-name-7 or integer-11}]]]

      [RECORDING MODE IS mode]

    [CODE SET IS alphabet-name-1].

REPORT FILE:

       FD file-name-1
            [IS EXTERNAL]

    [IS GLOBAL]
```

(continued)

(continued)

```
[BLOCK CONTAINS
   [integer-1 TO] integer-2
{RECORDS or CHARACTERS}]]

[RECORD
   {CONTAINS integer-3 CHARACTERS or
    CONTAINS integer-4 TO integer-5 CHARACTERS}]]

[LABEL {RECORD IS or RECORDS ARE}
   {STANDARD or OMITTED}]]

[VALUE OF {implementor-name-1 IS
   {data-name-2 or literal-1}}...]

[CODE SET IS alphabet-name-1]

{REPORT IS or REPORTS ARE}{report-name-1}....
```

DATA DESCRIPTION ENTRY

The DATA DESCRIPTION ENTRY SECTION describes the order
and hierarchy of the fields in each record of a file (*see also* Part IV
for more information):

FORMAT 1:

```
level-number [data-name-1 or FILLER]

[REDEFINES data-name-2]

[IS EXTERNAL]

[IS GLOBAL]

[{PICTURE or PIC} IS character-string]

  [[USAGE IS]
    {BINARY or COMPUTATIONAL or COMP or DISPLAY or INDEX
  or PACKED-DECIMAL}]

[[SIGN IS] {LEADING or TRAILING}[SEPARATE CHARACTER]]

  [OCCURS integer-2 TIMES
    [{ASCENDING or DESCENDING}
      KEY IS {data-name-3}...]...
    [INDEXED BY {index-name-1}...]
    OCCURS integer-1 TO integer-2 TIMES
      DEPENDING ON data-name-4 or
      [{ASCENDING or DESCENDING}
        KEY IS {data-name-3}...]...
      [INDEXED BY {index-name-1}...]]

[{SYNCHRONIZED or SYNC}[LEFT or RIGHT]]
```

[JUSTIFIED *or* JUST}RIGHT]

[BLANK WHEN ZERO]

[VALUE IS *literal-1*].

FORMAT 2:

66 *data-name-1* RENAMES *data-name-2*
  [{THROUGH *or* THRU} *data-name-3*].

FORMAT 3:

88 *condition-name-1* {VALUE IS *or* VALUES ARE}
  {*literal-1* [{THROUGH *or* THRU} *literal-2*]}.... *or*

{ NULL   or   NULLS }

COMMUNICATION DESCRIPTION ENTRY

The COMMUNICATION DESCRIPTION ENTRY SECTION defines data elements that are used when communicating with system devices (*see also* Part IV for more information):

FORMAT 1:

CD *cd-name-1*

  FOR [INITIAL] INPUT

    [[[SYMBOLIC QUEUE IS *data-name-1*]

        [SYMBOLIC SUB-QUEUE-1 IS *data-name-2*]

        [SYMBOLIC SUB-QUEUE-2 IS *data-name-3*]

        [SYMBOLIC SUB-QUEUE-3 IS *data-name-4*]

        [MESSAGE DATE IS *data-name-5*]

        [MESSAGE TIME IS *data-name-6*]

        [SYMBOLIC SOURCE IS *data-name-7*]

        [TEXT LENGTH IS *data-name-8*]

        [END KEY IS *data-name-9*]

        [STATUS KEY IS *data-name-10*]

        [MESSAGE COUNT IS *data-name-11*]]

(continued)

(continued)

```
        [data-name-1, data-name-2, data-name-3,     .
            data-name-4, data-name-5, data-name-6,
            data-name-7, data-name-8, data-name-9,
            data-name-10, data-name-11]].
```

FORMAT 2:

CD *cd-name-1* for OUTPUT

[DESTINATION COUNT IS *data-name-1*]

[TEXT LENGTH IS *data-name-2*]

[STATUS KEY IS *data-name-3*]

[DESTINATION TABLE OCCURS *integer-1* TIMES
    [INDEXED BY {*index-name-1*}...]]

   [ERROR KEY IS *data-name-4*]

   [SYMBOLIC DESTINATION IS *data-name-5*].

   [*data-name-1, data-name-2, data-name-3,*
       data-name-4, data-name-5]].

FORMAT 3:

CD *cd-name-1*

   FOR [INITIAL] I-O

      [[[MESSAGE DATE IS *data-name-1*]

         [MESSAGE TIME IS *data-name-2*]

         [SYMBOLIC TERMINAL IS *data-name-3*]

         [TEXT LENGTH IS *data-name-4*]

         [END KEY IS *data-name-5*]

         [STATUS KEY IS *data-name-6*]]

      [*data-name-1, data-name-2, data-name-3, data-name-4,*
         data-name-5, data-name-6]].

REPORT DESCRIPTION ENTRY

The REPORT DESCRIPTION ENTRY SECTION defines a report
and its associated data items (***see also*** Part IV for more information):

RD *report-name-1*

[IS GLOBAL]

```
[CODE literal-1]

   [{CONTROL IS or CONTROLS ARE}
    {{data-name-1}... or
   FINAL [data-name-1]...}]

   [PAGE [LIMIT IS or LIMITS ARE] integer-1
   [LINE or LINES][HEADING integer-2]

   [FIRST DETAIL integer-3][LAST DETAIL integer-4]

   [FOOTING integer-5]].
```

REPORT GROUP DESCRIPTION ENTRY

The REPORT GROUP DESCRIPTION ENTRY defines each group and detail item of a report, including headers and footers. The REPORT SECTION defines a report and its associated data items (*see also* Part IV for more information):

FORMAT 1:

01 [data-name-1]

```
   [LINE NUMBER IS {integer-1 [ON NEXT PAGE] or
                PLUS integer-2}]

   [NEXT GROUP IS {integer-3 or
                PLUS integer-4 or
             NEXT PAGE}]
```

TYPE IS

```
   {{REPORT HEADING or RH} or

   {PAGE HEADING or PH} or

   {CONTROL HEADING or CH} {data-name-2 or FINAL} or

   {DETAIL or DE} or

   {CONTROL FOOTING or CF} {data-name-3 or FINAL}

   {PAGE FOOTING or PF} or

   {REPORT FOOTING or RF}}

   [[USAGE IS] DISPLAY].
```

FORMAT 2:

level-number [data-name-1]

(continued)

(continued)

```
        [LINE NUMBER IS {integer-1 [ON NEXT PAGE] or
                        PLUS integer-2}]

            [[USAGE IS] DISPLAY].

    FORMAT 3:

    level-number [data-name-1]

    {PICTURE or PIC} IS character-string

            [[USAGE IS] DISPLAY]

    [[SIGN IS]{LEADING or TRAILING} SEPARATE CHARACTER]

    [{JUSTIFIED or JUST} RIGHT]

    [BLANK WHEN ZERO]

        [LINE NUMBER IS {integer-1 [ON NEXT PAGE] or
                        PLUS integer-2}]

    [COLUMN NUMBER IS integer-3]

  {SOURCE IS identifier-1 or

  VALUE IS literal-1 or

      {SUM {identifier-2}...[UPON {data-name-2}...]}... or
      [RESET ON {data-name-3 or FINAL}]]}

    [GROUP INDICATE].
```

PROCEDURE DIVISION

The PROCEDURE DIVISION is where the heart of a COBOL
program lies. This is where all the actual work gets done. As you
can tell from its name, the PROCEDURE DIVISION is where
procedures are defined. The PROCEDURE DIVISION has the
following syntax:

```
FORMAT 1:

[PROCEDURE DIVISION [USING {BY REFERENCE or VALUE}

    {data-name-1}...

                        RETURNING  {data-name-2}...].

[DECLARATIVES.

{section-name SECTION [segment-number].
```

```
USE statement.

[paragraph-name.

[sentence]...]...}...
```

END DECLARATIVES.]

```
{section-name SECTION [segment-number].

[paragraph-name.

[sentence]...]...}...]
```

FORMAT 2:

[PROCEDURE DIVISION [USING {data-name-1}...].

```
{paragraph-name.

[sentence]...}...]
```

COBOL Verbs

COBOL verbs define the step by step actions your COBOL programs will take, from verbs which open, read and process files, to verbs which add, divide, and multiply identifier values (**see also** Part VI for more information):

```
ACCEPT identifier-1 [FROM mnemonic-name-1]

ACCEPT identifier-2 FROM
   {DATE or DAY or DAY-OF-WEEK or TIME}

ACCEPT cd-name-1 MESSAGE COUNT

ADD {identifier-1 or literal-1}...
   TO {identifier-2 [ROUNDED]}...
[ON SIZE ERROR imperative-statement-1]
[NOT ON SIZE ERROR imperative-statement-2]
[END-ADD]

ADD {identifier-1 or literal-1}...
   TO {identifier-2 or literal-2}
GIVING {identifier-3 [ROUNDED]}...
[ON SIZE ERROR imperative-statement-1]
[NOT ON SIZE ERROR imperative-statement-2]
[END-ADD]

ADD {CORRESPONDING or CORR}
   identifier-1 TO identifier-2 [ROUNDED]
[ON SIZE ERROR imperative-statement-1]
[NOT ON SIZE ERROR imperative-statement-2]
```

(continued)

(continued)

```
[END-ADD]

ALTER {procedure-name-1 TO
  [PROCEED TO] procedure-name-2}...

CALL {identifier-1 or literal-1 or procedure-pointer-1}
  [USING {[BY REFERENCE] {identifier-2}... or
          BY CONTENT {identifier-2}...}...]
[ON OVERFLOW imperative-statement-1]
[END-CALL].

FORMAT 2:

CALL {identifier-1 or literal-1 or procedure-pointer-1}
  [USING {[BY REFERENCE] {identifier-2}... or
          BY CONTENT {identifier-2}...}...]
[ON EXCEPTION imperative-statement-1]
[NOT ON EXCEPTION imperative-statement-2]
[END-CALL].

CANCEL {identifier-1 or literal-1}...

CLOSE

  {file-name-1

    [{REEL or UNIT} [FOR REMOVAL] or

     WITH {NO REWIND or LOCK}]}...

CLOSE {file-name-1 [WITH LOCK]}...

COMPUTE {identifier-1 [ROUNDED]}...
  = arithmetic-expression-1
[ON SIZE ERROR imperative-statement-1]
[NOT ON SIZE ERROR imperative-statement-2]
[END-COMPUTE]

CONTINUE

DELETE file-name-1 RECORD
  [INVALID KEY imperative-statement-1]
[NOT INVALID KEY imperative-statement-2]
[END-DELETE]

DISABLE
  {INPUT [TERMINAL] or I-O TERMINAL or OUTPUT} cd-name-1
  [WITH KEY {identifier-1 or literal-1}]

DISPLAY {identifier-1 or literal-1}...
  [UPON mnemonic-name-1] [WITH NO ADVANCING]

DIVIDE {identifier-1 or literal-1}
  INTO {identifier-2 [ROUNDED]}...
  [ON SIZE ERROR imperative-statement-1]
```

```
  [NOT ON SIZE ERROR imperative-statement-2]
  [END-DIVIDE]

DIVIDE {identifier-1 or literal-1}
  INTO {identifier-2 or literal-2}
GIVING {identifier-3 [ROUNDED]}...
  [ON SIZE ERROR imperative-statement-1]
[NOT ON SIZE ERROR imperative-statement-2]
[END-DIVIDE].

DIVIDE {identifier-1 or literal-1}
  BY {identifier-2 or literal-2}
GIVING {identifier-3 [ROUNDED]}...
  [ON SIZE ERROR imperative-statement-1]
[NOT ON SIZE ERROR imperative-statement-2]
[END-DIVIDE]

DIVIDE {identifier-1 or literal-1}
  INTO {identifier-2 or literal-2}
  GIVING identifier-3 [ROUNDED]
REMAINDER identifier-4
  [ON SIZE ERROR imperative-statement-1]
[NOT ON SIZE ERROR imperative-statement-2]
[END-DIVIDE]

DIVIDE {identifier-1 or literal-1}
  BY {identifier-2 or literal-2}
GIVING {identifier-3 [ROUNDED]}...
REMAINDER identifier-4
  [ON SIZE ERROR imperative-statement-1]
[NOT ON SIZE ERROR imperative-statement-2]
[END-DIVIDE]

ENABLE
  {INPUT [TERMINAL] or I-O TERMINAL or OUTPUT} cd-name-1
  [WITH KEY {identifier-1 or literal-1}]

ENTER language-name-1 [routine-name-1].

EVALUATE
  {identifier-1 or literal-1 or expression-1
   or TRUE or FALSE}
  [ALSO {identifier-2 or literal-2 or expression-2
   or TRUE or FALSE}]...
  {{WHEN
    {ANY or
     condition-1 or
     TRUE or
     FALSE or
     [NOT] {{identifier-3 or
            literal-3 or
            arithmetic-expression-1}
          [{THROUGH or THRU}
           {identifier-4 or literal-4 or
            arithmetic-expression-2}]}}
```

(continued)

(continued)

```
[ALSO
    {ANY or
  condition-2 or
  TRUE or
  FALSE or
  [NOT]{{identifier-5 or
          literal-5 or
          arithmetic-expression-3}
        [{THROUGH or THRU}
         {identifier-6 or literal-6 or
          arithmetic-expression-4}]}}}]...}...
  imperative-statement-1}...
  [WHEN OTHER imperative-statement-2]
[END-EVALUATE]

EXIT

EXIT PROGRAM

GENERATE {data-name-1 or report-name-1}

GO TO [procedure-name-1]

GO TO {procedure-name-1}...DEPENDING ON identifier-1

IF condition-1
THEN {{statement-1}... or
      NEXT SENTENCE}
{ELSE {statement-2...[END-IF] or
      ELSE NEXT SENTENCE or
      END-IF}

INITIALIZE {identifier-1}...
[REPLACING
 {{ALPHABETIC or
   ALPHANUMERIC or
   NUMERIC or
   ALPHANUMERIC-EDITED or
   NUMERIC-EDITED}
DATA BY {identifier-2 or literal-1}}...]

INITIATE {report-name-1}...

INSPECT identifier-1 TALLYING
  {identifier-2 FOR
    {CHARACTERS [{BEFORE or AFTER} INITIAL
      {identifier-4 or literal-2}]... or
    {ALL or LEADING} {{identifier-3 or
                       literal-1} [{BEFORE or AFTER}
                       INITIAL {identifier-4 or
                                literal-2}]...}...}...}...

INSPECT identifier-1 REPLACING
  {CHARACTERS BY {identifier-5 or literal-3}
    [{BEFORE or AFTER} INITIAL
      {identifier-4 or literal-2}]... or
```

```
       {ALL or LEADING or FIRST} {{identifier-3 or literal-1}
          BY {identifier-5 or literal-3}
          [{BEFORE or AFTER} INITIAL
             {identifier-4 or literal-2}]...}...}...

    INSPECT identifier-1 TALLYING
       {identifier-2 FOR
          {CHARACTERS [{BEFORE or AFTER} INITIAL
             {identifier-4 or literal-2}]... or
          {ALL or LEADING}
             {{identifier-3 or literal-1}
             [{BEFORE or AFTER} INITIAL
                {identifier-4 or literal-2}]...}...}...}...
       REPLACING
          {CHARACTERS BY {identifier-5 or literal-3}
          [{BEFORE or AFTER} INITIAL
             {identifier-4 or literal-2}]... or
          {ALL or LEADING or FIRST}
                {{identifier-3 or literal-1} BY
                {identifier-5 or literal-3}
                [{BEFORE or AFTER} INITIAL
                   {identifier-4 or literal-2}]...}...}...

    INSPECT identifier-1 CONVERTING
       {identifier-6 or literal-4} TO
       {identifier-7 or literal-5}
       [{BEFORE or AFTER} INITIAL
          {identifier-4 or literal-2}]...

    MERGE file-name-1
       {ON {ASCENDING or DESCENDING} KEY {data-name-1}...}...
       [COLLATING SEQUENCE IS alphabet-name-1]
       USING file-name-2 {file-name-3}...
       {OUTPUT PROCEDURE IS procedure-name-1
          [{THROUGH or THRU} procedure-name-2] or
GIVING {file-name-4}...}

    MOVE {identifier-1 or literal-3} TO {identifier-2}...

    MOVE {CORRESPONDING or CORR} identifier-1 TO
       identifier-2

    MULTIPLY {identifier-1 or literal-1} BY
       {identifier-2 [ROUNDED]}...
       [ON SIZE ERROR imperative-statement-1]
       [NOT ON SIZE ERROR imperative-statement-2]
       [END-MULTIPLY]

    MULTIPLY {identifier-1 or literal-1} BY
       {identifier-2 or literal-2}
       GIVING {identifier-3} [ROUNDED]}...
       [ON SIZE ERROR imperative-statement-1]
       [NOT ON SIZE ERROR imperative-statement-2]
       [END-MULTIPLY]
```

(continued)

(continued)

```
OPEN
  {INPUT {file-name-1 [REVERSED or WITH NO REWIND]}... or
   OUTPUT {file-name-2 [WITH NO REWIND]}... or
   I-O {file-name-3}... or
   EXTEND {file-name-4}...}...

OPEN
  {INPUT {file-name-1}... or
   OUTPUT {file-name-2}... or
   I-O {file-name-3}... or
   EXTEND {file-name-4}...}...

OPEN
  {OUTPUT {file-name-1 [WITH NO REWIND]}... or
   EXTEND {file-name-2}...

PERFORM [procedure-name-1
  [{THROUGH or THRU} procedure-name-2]]
  [imperative-statement-1 END-PERFORM]

PERFORM [procedure-name-1
  [{THROUGH or THRU} procedure-name-2]]
  {identifier-1 or integer-1} TIMES
[imperative-statement-1 END-PERFORM]

PERFORM [procedure-name-1
  [{THROUGH or THRU} procedure-name-2]]
  [WITH TEST {BEFORE or AFTER}] UNTIL condition-1
[imperative-statement-1 END-PERFORM]

PERFORM [procedure-name-1
  [{THROUGH or THRU} procedure-name-2]]
  [WITH TEST {BEFORE or AFTER}]
    VARYING {identifier-4 or literal-1}
    FROM {identifier-3 or index-name-2 or literal-1}
    BY {identifier-4 or literal-2} UNTIL
      condition-1
    [AFTER {identifier-5 or index-name-3} FROM
      {identifier-6 or index-name-4 or literal-3}
    BY {identifier-7 or literal-4} UNTIL
      condition-2]...
  [imperative-statement-1 END-PERFORM]

PURGE cd-name-1

READ file-name-1 [NEXT] RECORD [INTO identifier-1]
[AT END imperative-statement-1]
[NOT AT END imperative-statement-2]
[END-READ]

READ file-name-1 RECORD [INTO identifier-1]
[INVALID KEY imperative-statement-1]
[NOT INVALID KEY imperative-statement-2]
[END-READ]
```

```
READ file-name-1 RECORD [INTO identifier-1]
[KEY IS data-name-1]
[INVALID KEY imperative-statement-1]
[NOT INVALID KEY imperative-statement-2]
[END-READ]

RECEIVE cd-name-1 {MESSAGE or SEGMENT} INTO identifier-1
[NO DATA imperative-statement-1]
[WITH DATA imperative-statement-2]
[END-RECEIVE]

RELEASE record-name-1 [FROM identifier-1]

RETURN file-name-1 RECORD [INTO identifier-1]
AT END imperative-statement-1
[NOT AT END imperative-statement-2]
[END-RETURN]

REWRITE record-name-1 [FROM identifier-1] [END-REWRITE]

REWRITE record-name-1 [FROM identifier-1]
[INVALID KEY imperative-statement-1]
[NOT INVALID KEY imperative-statement-2]
[END-REWRITE]

SEARCH identifier-1
  [VARYING {identifier-2 or index-name-1}]
[AT END imperative-statement-1]
  {WHEN condition-1
    {imperative-statement-2 or NEXT SENTENCE}}...
[END-SEARCH]

SEARCH ALL identifier-1
  [AT END imperative-statement-1]
  WHEN {data-name-1 {IS EQUAL TO or IS =}
      {identifier-3 or literal-1 or
       arithmetic-expression-1} or condition name-1}
    [AND {data-name-2 {IS EQUAL TO or IS =}
      {identifier-4 or literal-2 or
       arithmetic-expression-2} or condition-name-2}]...
  {imperative-statement-2 or NEXT SENTENCE}
[END-SEARCH]

SEND cd-name-1 FROM identifier-1

SEND cd-name-1 [FROM identifier-1]
  {WITH identifier-2 or
   WITH ESI or
   WITH EMI or
   WITH EGI}
  [{BEFORE or AFTER} ADVANCING
    {{identifier-3 or integer-1} [LINE or LINES] or
     {mnemonic-name-1 or PAGE}}]
[REPLACING LINE]
```

(continued)

(continued)

```
SET {index-name-1 or identifier-1}...
  TO {index-name-2 or identifier-2 or integer-1}

SET {index-name-3}...
  {UP BY or DOWN BY} {identifier-3 or integer-2}

SET {{mnemonic-name-1}...TO {ON or OFF}}...

SET {condition-name-1}...TO TRUE

SORT file-name-1
  {ON {ASCENDING or DESCENDING} KEY {data-name-1}...}...
[WITH DUPLICATES IN ORDER]
[COLLATING SEQUENCE IS alphabet-name-1]
  {INPUT PROCEDURE IS procedure-name-1
    [{THROUGH or THRU} procedure-name-2] or
    USING {file-name-2}...
  {OUTPUT PROCEDURE IS procedure-name-3
    [{THROUGH or THRU} procedure-name-4] or
GIVING {file-name-3}...

START file-name-1
  [KEY {IS EQUAL TO or
        IS = or
        IS GREATER THAN or
        IS > or
        IS NOT LESS THAN or
        IS NOT < or
        IS GREATER THAN OR EQUAL TO or
        IS >=} data-name-1]
[INVALID KEY imperative-statement-1]
[NOT INVALID KEY imperative-statement-2]
[END-START]

STOP {RUN or literal-1}

STRING {{identifier-1 or literal-1}...
  DELIMITED BY {identifier-2 or literal-2 or SIZE}}...
  INTO identifier-3
[WITH POINTER identifier-4]
[ON OVERFLOW imperative-statement-1]
[NOT ON OVERFLOW imperative-statement-2]
[END-STRING]

SUBTRACT {identifier-1 or literal-1}...
  FROM {identifier-2 [ROUNDED]}...
  [ON SIZE ERROR imperative-statement-1]
[NOT ON SIZE ERROR imperative-statement-2]
[END-SUBTRACT]

SUBTRACT {identifier-1 or literal-1}...
  FROM {identifier-2 or literal-2}
  GIVING {identifier-3 [ROUNDED]}...
  [ON SIZE ERROR imperative-statement-1]
```

```
[NOT ON SIZE ERROR imperative-statement-2]
[END-SUBTRACT]

SUBTRACT {CORRESPONDING or CORR} identifier-1
  FROM {identifier-2 [ROUNDED]}...
  [ON SIZE ERROR imperative-statement-1]
[NOT ON SIZE ERROR imperative-statement-2]
[END-SUBTRACT]

SUPPRESS PRINTING

TERMINATE {report-name-1}...

UNSTRING identifier-1
  [DELIMITED BY [ALL]
    {identifier-2 or literal-1}
    [OR [ALL] {identifier-3 or literal-2}]...]
  INTO {identifier-4 [DELIMITER IN identifier-5]
    [COUNT IN identifier-6]}...
[WITH POINTER identifier-7]
[TALLYING IN identifier-8]
[ON OVERFLOW imperative-statement-1]
[NOT ON OVERFLOW imperative-statement-2]
[END-UNSTRING]

USE [GLOBAL] AFTER STANDARD
  {EXCEPTION or ERROR} PROCEDURE ON
  {{file-name-1}... or INPUT or OUTPUT or I-O or EXTEND}

USE AFTER STANDARD

  {EXCEPTION or ERROR} PROCEDURE ON

  {{file-name-1}... or OUTPUT or EXTEND}

USE [GLOBAL] BEFORE REPORTING identifier-1

USE FOR DEBUGGING ON
  {cd-name-1 or
  [ALL REFERENCES OF] identifier-1 or file-name-1 or
  procedure-name-1 or ALL PROCEDURES}...

WRITE record-name-1 [FROM identifier-1]
  [{BEFORE or AFTER} ADVANCING
  {{identifier-2 or integer-1} [LINE or LINES] or
  {mnemonic-name-1 or
  PAGE}}]
[AT {END-OF-PAGE or EOP} imperative-statement-1]
[NOT AT {END-OF-PAGE or EOP} imperative-statement-2]
[END-WRITE]

WRITE record-name-1 [FROM identifier-1]
[INVALID KEY imperative-statement-1]
[NOT INVALID KEY imperative-statement-2]
[END-WRITE]
```

Conditions

A condition is a logical expression that can be assigned a truth value. Conditions control the executing of your program, based on the value or type of a variable or identifier.

RELATION CONDITION:

```
{identifier-1 or
 literal-1 or
 arithmetic-expression-1 or
 index-name-1}
{IS [NOT] GREATER THAN or
 IS [NOT] > or
 IS [NOT] LESS THAN or
 IS [NOT] < or
 IS [NOT] EQUAL TO or
 IS [NOT] = or
 IS GREATER THAN OR EQUAL TO or
 IS >= or
 IS LESS THAN OR EQUAL TO or
 IS <=}
{identifier-2 or
 literal-2 or
 arithmetic-expression-2 or
index-name-2}
```

CLASS CONDITION:

```
identifier-1 IS [NOT]
  {NUMERIC or
   ALPHABETIC or
   ALPHABETIC-LOWER or
   ALPHABETIC-UPPER or
class-name-1}
```

CONDITION-NAME-CONDITION:

```
condition-name-1
```

SWITCH-STATUS CONDITION:

```
condition-name-1
```

SIGN CONDITION:

```
arithmetic-expression-1 IS [NOT]
{POSITIVE or NEGATIVE or ZERO}
```

NEGATED CONDITION:

```
NOT condition-1
```

COMBINED CONDITION:

```
condition-1 {{AND or OR} condition-2}...
```

ABBREVIATED COMBINED RELATION CONDITION:

>   *relation-condition* {{**AND** *or* **OR**} [**NOT**]
>   [*relation-operator*] *object*}...

Qualification

Qualifiers refer to data items, condition names, procedure names, or text names in an application.

Data-name Qualification

>   *data-name-1* [{**IN** *or* **OF**} *data-name-2*]...
>   [{**IN** *or* **OF**}
>   {*cd-name-1 or file-name-1 or report-name-1*}]

Condition-name-Qualification

condition-name-1 {{{**IN** *or* **OF**} *data-name-1*}...

[{**IN** *or* **OF**}

{*file-name-1 or cd-name-1*}] *or*

{**IN** *or* **OF**} {*file-name-1 or cd-name-1*}}

Procedure Qualification

>   *paragraph-name-1* {**IN** *or* **OF**} *section-name-1*

Text-name Qualification

>   *text-name-1* {**IN** *or* **OF**} *library-name-1*

Linage-counter Qualification

>   **LINAGE COUNTER** {**IN** *or* **OF**} *file-name-2*

Page-counter and Line-counter Qualification

>   {**PAGE-COUNTER** *or* **LINE-COUNTER**}
>   {**IN** *or* **OF**} *report-name-1*

Data-name in Report Qualification

>   *data-name-1*
>   {{**IN** *or* **OF**} *data-name-2*
>   [{**IN** *or* **OF**} *report-name-1*] *or*
>   {**IN** *or* **OF**} *report-name-1*}

Other

A few other grab bag formats appear in COBOL programs, including how to specify a table item subscript, reference a character in a data item, and how to qualify a table item.

SUBSCRIPTING:

```
{condition-name-1 or data-name-1}
({integer-1 or
   data-name-2
[{+} integer-2 or index-name-1 [{+} integer-3]}...)
```

REFERENCE:

data-name-1 (left-character-position: [length])

IDENTIFIER:

```
data-name-1 [{IN or OF} data-name-2]...
            [{IN or OF} {cd-name-1 or file-name-1 or
                          report-name-1}]
  [({subscript}...)] [(leftmost-character-position:
  [length])]
```

Index

T

Y

Year 2000
  Internet resources, 184–186
  planning your project, 176–178
  solving problems, 175–186
  testing and integration, 182–184
  update programs, 178–180
year-2000 compliant, definition, 178

Z

ZERO sign condition, 83–84

IDG BOOKS WORLDWIDE BOOK REGISTRATION

Register This Book and Win!

We want to hear from you!

Visit **http://my2cents.dummies.com** to register this book and tell us how you liked it!

- Get entered in our monthly prize giveaway.

- Give us feedback about this book — tell us what you like best, what you like least, or maybe what you'd like to ask the author and us to change!

- Let us know any other ...*For Dummies* topics that interest you.

Your feedback helps us determine what books to publish, tells us what coverage to add as we revise our books, and lets us know whether we're meeting your needs as a ...*For Dummies* reader. You're our most valuable resource, and what you have to say is important to us!

Not on the Web yet? It's easy to get started with *Dummies 101®: The Internet For Windows® 95* or *The Internet For Dummies®,* 4th Edition, at local retailers everywhere.

Or let us know what you think by sending us a letter at the following address:

...*For Dummies* Book Registration
Dummies Press
7260 Shadeland Station, Suite 100
Indianapolis, IN 46256
Fax 317-596-5498

BUSINESS AND
GENERAL
REFERENCE
BOOK SERIES
FROM IDG

COMPUTER
BOOK SERIES
FROM IDG